About the Author
Michael Keating is a journalist and photographer who has been active as both an alpine and cross-country skier since childhood. His columns on skiing have appeared regularly in several newspapers. Keating has recently travelled to a wide range of ski areas across Canada to write feature articles for *The Globe & Mail.*

Cross-Country Ontario

Michael Keating

Foreword by Jack Rabbit Johannsen

Endorsed by the Canadian Ski Association

Van Nostrand Reinhold Ltd., Toronto
New York, Cincinnati, London, Melbourne

Copyright ©.1979 by Michael Keating

All rights reserved. No part of this work covered by the copyrights hereon may be reproduced or used in any form or by any means — graphic, electronic, or mechanical, including photocopying, recording, taping or information storage and retrieval systems — without the prior written permission of the publisher.

Cover Photograph: Simon Hoyle

Printed and bound in Canada by The Alger Press Limited
Library of Congress Catalogue Number 79-66494

CANADIAN CATALOGUING IN PUBLICATION DATA

Keating, Michael, 1943-
  Cross-country Ontario

ISBN 0-442-29781-5

1. Cross-country skiing – Ontario – Guide-books.
2. Ontario – Description and travel – Guide-books.
I. Title.

GV854.9.C7K4	796.9'3'09713	C79-094616-5

79 80 81 82 83 84 85 86 8 7 6 5 4 3 2 1

To Doretta Keating

Contents

Foreword *IX*

Preface *XI*

Introduction *XII*

Basic Equipment *1*
Skis, Boots, Bindings, Poles, Clothing, Accessories, Quality and Cost

Basic Technique *9*
Starting Off, Advanced Skiing, Waxing, Conditioning

Touring and Winter Camping *17*
Wilderness Skiing, Camping Equipment, Checklists, Eating Out

Navigation *27*
Basic Tools, Orienteering Skills

Winter Survival *35*
Equipment, Shelter, Keeping Warm, Fire, Accidents and First Aid

The Elements of Winter *45*
Snow, Ice, Weather

Winter Photography *55*

Car and Skier *57*

Southern Ontario Trails *61*
1 Windsor – Sarnia Area   *61*
2 London Area   *61*
3 Goderich Area   *63*
4 Bruce Peninsula   *63*
5 Grey – Bruce Area   *66*
6 Kitchener – Waterloo Area   *67*
7 Niagara Peninsula   *67*
8 Greater Toronto Area   *69*
9 Oshawa Area   *72*
10 Orangeville – Bradford Area   *73*
11 Nottawasaga Bay   *74*
12 Muskoka   *77*
13 Algonquin   *79*
14 Haliburton   *81*
15 Peterborough – Kawarthas Area   *82*
16 Belleville Area   *86*
17 Kingston – Rideau Area   *88*
18 St. Lawrence Valley   *89*
19 Lower Ottawa Valley   *90*
20 Upper Ottawa Valley   *93*

Northern Ontario Trails *95*
1 North Bay – Temagami Area *95*
2 Kirkland Lake Area *97*
3 Sudbury Area *98*
4 Timmins – Hearst Area *100*
5 Algoma – Sault Area *101*
6 North Shore Area *103*
7 Thunder Bay – Quetico Area *104*
8 Dryden – Fort Frances *106*

Appendix *108*
Wind Chill Factors *108*
Time Required to Ski a Given Distance at Different Speeds *108*
Speed of Travel in Different Activities *109*
Canadian Ski Association *110*
Ski Trail Signs *111*
Metric Conversion Table *111*

Foreword

This book will be welcomed by every cross-country skier who seeks health and recreation through this greatest of all outdoor sports. It will help both expert and beginner to strike out with confidence into our wonderful Canadian wilderness, using equipment adapted to comfortable travel in rough or easy country and on any kind of snow.

When I was an active competitor in Norway during the early 1890's, we used the same pair of skis for slalom, downhill, jumping and cross-country, and our crowning achievement was the 50-kilometre race. An entirely new course was laid out for each competition, over deliberately difficult terrain and often under varying snow conditions. Since no competitor was allowed to run the course before the official start, each participant had to draw upon the agility he had learned in slalom, the courage he had acquired in straight downhill running, and the balance necessary for jumping. The 50-kilometre race was much more than proof of prolonged endurance. It was a real test of all-round skiing ability.

Since that time I have retained a keen interest in skiing, and have had a good deal to do with the development of the sport in a number of countries.

It is a sad fact that whenever any sport comes into vogue, it is not long before it is commercially exploited. It is no surprise, therefore, that when slalom and downhill became increasingly popular in the 1940's, both disciplines fell easy prey to big business. Enormous sums of money were spent on costly facilities which included chair lifts, artificial snow, and the usual complement of bars, restaurants and satellite industries. At the same time, individual equipment became highly specialized. Exaggerated boots, heavy skis and safety bindings made their appearance. These were designed for faster and faster speeds on mechanically groomed slalom and downhill slopes, but were impossible to manoeuvre independently on the level or for uphill climbing. The skier became a virtual slave of his equipment, and what had been a simple sport soon became an expensive racket.

But the pendulum is now swinging back. Today, some 30 years later, many skiers are tiring of the crowded slopes. They long for the wide open spaces away from the herd. And what do they find? The exploiters are already lying in wait for them with more specialized equipment and with artificially scored tracks, this time to accommodate extra light-weight skis, which are totally useless if the skier is forced off the path into deep snow. The developers are, in fact, trying to turn cross-country skiing (which has been a normal means of winter transportation in Norway for 4,000 years) into yet another kind of money-making rat race. They are marketing skis in proliferating styles, many of them quite unadaptable to varying conditions. In eliminating weight, they often sacrifice strength. They ignore the fact that the key to the real joy of ski-touring lies in dependable, durable, simple equipment with which one can leave the beaten trail and skim the fresh snow, penetrating with minimum effort into new and untrampled territory.

That is why I like this book. It takes the mystery out of cross-country skiing. It opens up untold possibilities for healthy winter enjoyment. It stimulates independence, resourcefulness and initiative in the individual, and it stresses our collective responsibility towards the snowy environment on which our sport depends.

Read this book. Digest it. And then get out on your skis. The hills are waiting! Good luck.

"Chief Jack Rabbit"
H. Smith-Johannsen

Preface

Cross-country skiing has come of age in Ontario. Just a few years ago we discovered that we have a perfect terrain and climate for the sport. Since then thousands of people a year have bought their first cross-country skis and cut their first tracks in snow close to home. Now they are joining the more seasoned skiers in looking further afield for something a bit longer, wilder or just different. *Cross-Country Ontario* has trail and skiing information for skiers of all ages and abilities.

The first section simply and clearly explains the basics of such things as ski equipment and technique, winter camping and route finding. The next section lists 287 trails for anything from an afternoon's outing in a nearby park to a wilderness adventure in Northern Ontario.

This book is based on *Cross-Country Canada*, the first book to list cross-country ski trails from coast to coast. *Cross-Country Ontario* was written after the completion of a survey to update trail information and to locate almost 100 new trails created in the past three years. Most of the trail information was provided in response to questionnaires by persons responsible for the routes. In some cases trail maps and more specific information are available from sources listed with the trails.

Those of you who have read the first book may notice some names missing in the new trail list. Several of these deletions point to signs of our times. One reason is a cutback in government spending, and some trails have been closed for lack of maintenance. A second and more disturbing reason was revealed in letters from some parks officials who wanted their small conservation areas deleted from the new book. They said some nature reserves are already so overcrowded that they are trying not to attract any more skiers. With great reluctance I agreed to their requests.

This preface would not be complete if I did not try to thank people who have helped me prepare the book. In particular I want to thank Mike Exall, director of the Centre of Outdoor Pursuits at Seneca College, King City. I would also like to thank Jack Rabbit Johannsen not only for writing the foreword but also for the inspiration he has provided me as a fellow skier. People in the Ministry of Natural Resources, the Conservation Authorities and Parks Canada have been very helpful in digging out information for me. In addition I want to thank all the many other people across Ontario who took the time to answer my requests for information and who often included notes of encouragement and even hand-drawn maps of their areas.

To you all: Good Skiing.

M. K.

Introduction

The rolling, often forested countryside of Ontario has been favorably compared with the classic ski terrain of the Nordic countries which developed cross-country skiing. For many years this fact was ignored by all but a handful of devotees. Though records show that Lord Frederick Hamilton, a British aide-de-camp to the Governor-General, skied near Ottawa in 1887, relatively few residents of the province followed in his tracks.

It was not really until the early 1970s that the sport caught hold in this province. There was already a substantial corps of downhill skiers and considerable interest in the sport of skiing generally when what is called the cross-country boom began. In the space of a few years tens of thousands of residents had taken up the sport. With a population of over 8 million, Ontario is a region with tremendous potential for development. At first the new skiers had a limited selection of trails, but that picture is changing rapidly. Downhill ski resort operators, for example, were quick to respond and most have by now blazed at least a couple of trails from their base lodges.

Ski clubs, especially those with a Nordic bent, also became more active and they are responsible for many of the free trails which have been cut across public and private lands. These provide some of the best touring in the province. Since they often cross private property it is essential skiers show the utmost respect for the land and avoid leaving any garbage, cutting wood or setting fires unless there are specific fire areas officially marked. Otherwise the trails may be closed.

The third major source of trails is the hiking clubs such as the Bruce Trail Association and its younger sisters, which have trails suitable for skiing. One cannot automatically assume he can ski any hiking trail for these routes sometimes make precipitous climbs not feasible on skis or even on foot in the winter, but there are usually skiable sections of trails. Finding them requires personal research or information from the trail club.

Ontario's ski trail system is still at a relatively early stage of development. Though there are thousands of kilometres of marked or mapped routes, this province has not quite reached the sophisticated stage of, for example, the Laurentians in Québec, where trail systems connect to allow extensive trips. Ontario skiers must usually return to their starting point or camp out overnight, but there are indications that trail systems will start meeting and linking such points as hotels and overnight shelters in a region.

Government agencies have thousands of square kilometres of potentially skiable land under their jurisdiction but relatively little of it has been cut and marked for such travel. The agencies seem to be responding to the ever-growing public demand for trails with a steady increase in marked routes and in other cases are aiding private ski clubs which are laying out trail systems on public land.

In Northern Ontario winter ski camps, many of them based at summer canoe lodges, are starting to draw skiers seeking weekend or week-long snow adventures. Groups make day trips from rustic hotels or overnight outings with tents and sleeping bags.

With an area of more than one million square kilometres, Ontario is the second largest province and by far the most heavily populated. The northern section of the province, an area of endless kilometres of lakes, rivers and boreal forest on the Canadian Shield, is a sparsely populated region but has fantastic skiing potential. There are thousands of kilometres of trails that follow logging, mining and summer cottage access roads.

By contrast the small southern section, ranging from Shield land to hardwood forests and rolling farm land, is densely populated. A large portion of it falls within a rich agricultural area of intensive mixed farming, fruit orchards and livestock grazing land. Where the fields end the subdivisions begin in many parts of the region, which helps to explain why many of the trail systems are so short. They are often located on woodlots or forest reserves intended for preservation of timber and for recreation.

Generally skiers in Southern Ontario can count on a season starting in December, usually around Christmas, and lasting until late March or early April. Even within the south the season may vary by a month, as Toronto skiers who drive north to the Muskoka region realize. In the north the season is even longer. Local weather patterns and temperatures tend to vary widely because of the moderating effect of winds passing over the Great Lakes and creating localized storms along the shorelines.

As befits a province with a burgeoning ski population, Ontario has some big ski events each year. There are three main ski races, which are open to all.

Muskoka Loppet — Started in the early 1970s this race has become one of the biggest in Canada and draws a couple of thousand entries each year. It is usually held in early January and run over a 30 km course from Hidden Valley, east of Huntsville, to Port Sydney on Mary Lake. While racers may finish the course in half a day, skiers usually take most of the daylight hours to make the trip through Muskoka countryside. For those seeking a shorter test of their skills there are 7.5 and 15 km courses laid out from Port Sydney. Scandinavian immigrants or descendants have added such Nordic touches to the event as pine garlands and blueberry soup. For information write Muskoka Loppet, Box 1239, Huntsville, Ont.

Silver Spoon Grand Prix — This started as a local race in Deep River in 1973 but now draws entrants, including racers preparing for the Canadian Marathon, from Quebec and from Ontario points as far away as Sault Ste. Marie and Toronto. The event is part of festivities on the second weekend of February, with competitions Saturday and tours in the nearby Petawawa Forest Experiment Station on Sunday.

The race has an interesting history. In the fall of 1972 two Deep River skiers, Aston Eikrem and Henry Hollo, were clearing a ski trail near the town and trying to think of a name for it when Aston's two-year-old son, Andreas, found a silver spoon lying in some bushes. That spoon gave the trail its name and became the symbol of a regular ski race. Now the fastest man over a 15 km course and the fastest woman over a 10 km course win silver spoons as trophies. For information write: Mike Watson, Box 770, Deep River, Ont., R0J 1P0.

Kawartha Ski Tour — Also preceding the Marathon is the Peterborough area tour which offers a challenge to all levels of skier. The trail starts at the village of Apsley, 50 km (30 mi.) north of Peterborough on Hwy. 28. From there it follows the course of Eel's Creek south to the hamlet of Haultain, then bears west through rugged country near the Burleigh Ridge and across Long Marshland. This is a wilderness trail with a great variety of skiing. The event is usually held in the middle of February and is organized in sections so skiers of all levels can find a route that matches their abilities. While racers may cover the 60 km course in a day, less seasoned skiers may opt to do it over the weekend or to ski one section only. Busing is arranged to shuttle skiers to and from their cars. In the past registration has been limited to the first 400 skiers. For information write: Kawartha Tourist Assn., Box 802, Peterborough, Ont.

In addition to these and a growing number of similar races, loppets and mara-

		Mean Temperature In Celsius (Fahrenheit)		Snowfall In Mean Centimetres (Inches)
		Min	Max	
Toronto	Dec	- 7.3 (18.8)	.3 (32.6)	27.9 (11.0)
	Jan	-10.5 (13.1)	- 2.2 (28.1)	35.1 (13.8)
	Feb	-10.3 (13.5)	- 1.4 (29.5)	30.0 (11.8)
	Mar	- 5.2 (22.6)	3.3 (38.0)	22.1 (8.7)
Ottawa	Dec	-11.6 (11.1)	- 3.7 (25.3)	51.6 (20.3)
	Jan	-15.6 (4.0)	- 6.4 (20.5)	48.5 (19.1)
	Feb	14.4 (6.1)	- 4.7 (23.5)	47.8 (18.8)
	Mar	- 7.5 (18.5)	1.3 (34.4)	35.1 (13.8)
North Bay	Dec	-13.1 (8.4)	- 4.1 (24.7)	51.3 (20.2)
	Jan	-17.9 (- 0.2)	- 6.7 (20.0)	51.1 (20.1)
	Feb	-16.3 (2.6)	- 4.4 (24.0)	41.9 (16.5)
	Mar	-10.1 (13.9)	1.6 (34.9)	29.0 (11.4)
Sault Ste Marie	Dec	-11.1 (12.0)	- 2.9 (26.8)	55.4 (21.8)
	Jan	-14.3 (6.3)	- 4.7 (23.6)	65.0 (25.6)
	Feb	-14.3 (6.2)	- 4.4 (24.0)	51.3 (20.2)
	Mar	- 9.9 (14.1)	.5 (32.9)	38.1 (15.0)
Huntsville	Dec	-11.5 (11.3)	- 2.3 (27.9)	71.6 (28.2)
	Jan	-15.3 (4.4)	- 4.6 (23.8)	71.6 (28.2)
	Feb	-14.3 (6.3)	- 2.7 (27.1)	55.4 (21.8)
	Mar	- 9.4 (15.0)	2.1 (35.8)	42.9 (16.9)
London	Dec	- 7.? (19.1)	0.0 (32.0)	47.2 (18.6)
	Jan	- 9.9 (14.2)	- 2.2 (28.0)	49.0 (19.3)
	Feb	- 9.7 (14.5)	- 1.6 (29.2)	40.9 (16.1)
	Mar	- 5.0 (23.0)	3.4 (38.2)	26.9 (10.6)
Thunder Bay	Dec	-15.9 (3.4)	- 5.6 (21.9)	45.5 (17.9)
	Jan	-20.7 (- 5.2)	- 8.9 (16.0)	51.6 (20.3)
	Feb	-19.7 (- 3.5)	- 6.2 (20.8)	31.0 (12.2)
	Mar	-12.3 (9.9)	0.0 (32.0)	35.3 (13.9)
Peterborough	Dec	- 9.9 (14.2)	- 1.6 (29.2)	34.0 (13.4)
	Jan	-13.4 (7.9)	- 3.7 (25.3)	39.9 (15.7)
	Feb	-12.6 (9.3)	- 2.4 (27.7)	37.3 (14.7)
	Mar	- 6.9 (19.5)	2.9 (37.3)	21.1 (8.3)
Collingwood	Dec	- 7.3 (18.8)	- 0.3 (31.5)	69.1 (27.2)
	Jan	-10.3 (13.5)	- 2.3 (27.8)	68.6 (27.0)
	Feb	-10.3 (13.5)	- 1.9 (28.6)	43.4 (17.1)
	Mar	- 6.0 (21.2)	2.9 (36.7)	31.8 (12.5)

thons there are other winter events which often interest skiers visiting or living in a given region. For example, there is a growing number of winter carnivals, often with ski races as part of the festivities.

The provincial government has a comprehensive winter information program which provides skiers with snow reports. This is located at the Barrie Travel Centre (705) 726-0932 or 728-5851. Skiers in Toronto can call toll free at 364-4722. In addition most newspapers and radio stations and a number of television stations carry snow reports. Information on driving conditions during the winter can be obtained from (416) 248-3561 in Toronto.

Booklets giving lists of downhill and cross-country ski resorts, snowmobile areas and winter parks as well as a Winter Events booklet are published each year and are available from the Ministry of Industry and Tourism, Queen's Park, Toronto, Ont. The Ministry of Natural Resources, Information Office, Queen's Park, also has a useful booklet called Winter Recreation on Public Lands, which simply indicates places such as parks, public forests and conservation areas where cross-country skiing can be practiced. Lodging information is often available through ski resorts or chambers of commerce in particular towns or regions but a province-wide handbook is Accommodations Ontario, also from the Ministry of Industry and Tourism.

Basic Equipment

One of the great pleasures of cross-country skiing is the light, graceful equipment. Particularly for people used to the heavy, sometimes cumbersome gear developed for downhill runs, the slender skis and low-cut boots developed for gliding over the snow can be a revelation. And cross-country outfits are delightfully simple.

The delicate lines of the skis are broken only by small, metal bindings which clamp the toes of the low, leather boots in a firm grip but leave the heels free to rise and fall in a natural stride. Poles are long, slender wands to be rhythmically swung and leaned upon as the skier slips across the frozen countryside. Suitable clothing means something loose and relatively light in weight, since the constantly moving skier generates a steady flow of body heat.

Another pleasure of cross-country outfits is the relatively low cost — especially in comparison to the expensive downhill material. As a rough minimum you should count on spending about seventy-five dollars for a cross-country package: decent wood skis with aluminium bindings, leather boots and bamboo poles. A comfortable outfit can be made from long johns, jeans, sweaters and a nylon jacket, but as time goes on you will most likely want a pair of the comfortable knicker pants and possibly a matching jacket with such features as a windproof front, stretch inserts and zippered pockets.

There are a few rules to remember when buying equipment, especially a whole outfit. The first is to take time to find out what you need and to get it properly fitted. In other words, don't hit the first ski shop on the street after five on Friday and expect to walk out of the place properly outfitted by closing time. You'll probably need at least an hour to choose a pair of skis. If ski fever hits you overnight, go to a nearby resort on Saturday morning — early Saturday morning — rent equipment and take a lesson. In any case, renting is not a bad idea since it lets you try the sport for a few dollars.

Even if you feel ready for the salesman take a bit more time to ask some other skiers and several ski shop people for advice on what equipment sold in your area would suit your needs. Shop around as long as you're at it. Many stores will offer a discount if you buy a package and most have sales before and after the peak season. These days competition is so fierce that there seem to be ski sales at every time except Christmas. If you know what you want, keep an eye out for ski swaps run by local clubs. Sometimes there are genuine bargains among the battle-scarred relics.

A word about discount and mail-order houses. Know what you are after and what size you need. In the case of the mails there will be a long wait if you make a mistake and some discount houses economize so much on staff that you practically have to serve yourself. The advantage of a specialty ski shop is that it usually houses some expertise, but again make sure your salesman is not just a downhill specialist or a tennis bum sitting out the winter. Ask some pointed questions; for example, what kind of skis does he use and why does he think Brand X is best for you?

Once you latch onto a good salesman, give him a good idea of your ability and ambitions so he can advise you well.

Skis

Believe it or not, the wide, stubby skis used by many downhill skiers and the long, narrow skis for cross-country trips have a common origin. Skis seem to have first evolved in the northern parts of Scandinavia and Siberia in various combinations, including pairs in which a short ski was used for pushing and a long one for gliding. During the last century, the skis brought to North America by Scandinavian immigrants were each the same length and two or three feet longer than the skier was tall. This type of ski, a board planed, sanded and then steamed so the tip could be bent up, was used as late as the 1950s. About the only place you see them now is over the mantels of fireplaces in ski lodges.

Over the past several centuries downhill skiing as a specialty evolved slowly — perhaps because until ski lifts were developed in the 1930s, the equipment still had to allow for skiers to walk and climb back up hills. With the advent of lifts and crowds, ski slopes became hard packed and strong, heavy skis with steel edges were introduced for the downhill runs. On the other hand, cross-country skis were being made even slimmer and lighter for speeding along tracks in the snow. Now a pair of light touring skis weighs and costs about half as much as its downhill equivalent.

In this century manufacturers started gluing different types of wood together to get the best combination of strength, springiness and durability from a wood ski. Good laminated skis can have as many as thirty-five strips of wood sandwiched together. Despite the arrival of metal and fiberglass materials, wood skis are still a good investment and offer a few advantages.

In addition to the beauty of well-varnished wood, you can count a price advantage and the fact that wood is still the best base material for cross-country skiing. No synthetic will directly take wax as well as a wood base or continue to grip the snow as well once the wax wears thin. Some people take satisfaction in caring for wood and develop a rapport with the skis as they carefully soften pine tar with a torch and rub it into the bases each year to waterproof the wood.

But in cross-country as in downhill equipment, fiberglass is likely to take over in the next few years. Synthetics are generally stronger and they are virtually immune to warping if carelessly stored. You can get a quite decent pair of wood skis for about forty dollars, and seventy dollars or so should buy the best of that type. Fiberglass skis start at about that range and can cost more than one hundred dollars.

Ski sole or base design is still in a state of flux. On the one hand there is the classic wood surface which must be waterproofed periodically with pine tar but which holds wax well. Then there are the various types of smooth plastic bases found on all synthetic and some wood skis. They don't need tarring against wetness, but they do need more careful waxing than wood to achieve the proper grip.

There is some experimentation with slippery plastics such as P-Tex used on downhill skis. The theory is that the plastic will provide all the glide necessary and a small amount of sticky wax will give the grip needed to get moving.

For several years there have been moderately successful attempts to eliminate waxing completely by designing a sole which will both grip the snow and allow gliding. The major designs are either a step or fish scale-like pattern in the plastic or strips of short bristles, often referred to as Fiber-Tran or Mohair. However, these designs are not as effective in all types of snow as waxes and they are usually recommended for casual skiers.

No matter what the color, construction or base design, the key factor in choosing the right type of cross-country ski is width. Basically there are four types: mountain, touring, light touring and racing. Any ski wider than 60 mm (about 2 ½ inches) at the centre is considered a mountain-type ski and is best suited for people who climb high hills and make long runs in all types of snow conditions. These are virtually downhill skis and are unsuited for the kick and glide motions which propel cross-country skiers over flat ground.

Next in size is the touring ski, the widest true cross-country ski. With a width of about 55 mm under the bindings, touring skis are big enough to float over unbroken snow and strong enough to handle the sometimes abrupt changes of terrain one finds while bushwhacking off the beaten track. This is a good ski for someone who will be skiing both on and off prepared trails and might carry the occasional pack or wander into hilly terrain where the descents won't be too steep for wide, gentle turns.

Slimmest of the general purpose skis are the light touring models, which are about 50 mm wide at the waist. Though not as strong, stable or good at floating over soft snow, the light touring models are livelier and faster. Many recreational skiers, especially those who will usually be skiing tracks made by other skiers, choose them for lightness and speed, and some professionals even use them in the bush and mountainous terrain.

The narrowest skis– 40 to 50 mm– are the racing models. These slender boards are meant specifically for flashing along prepared tracks and are not suitable for all-round use. Choosing the right width of ski is simply a matter of deciding what type of skiing you want to do.

Choosing the right length is also fairly easy. There is the classic method of raising your arm straight up and picking a ski that comes to about your wrist or palm. Then there is the more recent paper test in which you stand on a ski on a flat surface and should just be able to pull a sheet of paper from under the mid-point. Many ski shops have simple charts which correlate height and weight of purchasers to the correct ski length.

Boots
Just as there are four general types of skis there are four boot types to give the right degree of flexibility and control. You need something like a hiking boot to muscle around a mountain ski, while the racing boot is like a lightweight track shoe. The touring and light touring boots are also quite light and flexible to allow a good stride.

In cross-country boots, more than anywhere else in the sport, tradition is hanging on. Though synthetic soles have almost completely replaced leather, natural material is still the best for the uppers. Its unique advantages are that it remains supple at all temperatures and it breathes– allowing perspiration to escape from around your feet. Until a synthetic with these properties is discovered and produced at a reasonable price, we will continue to be best shod in leather.

Leather, like wood, is sensitive to moisture over a period of time and needs some protection. Boots should be regularly treated with wax or shoe polish and should be waterproofed with silicone or a paste called Sno-Seal. If you are skiing in very wet conditions, such as in the spring, consider a pair of neoprene overboots sold in ski shops.

When you are buying boots you should expect to pay thirty dollars and up for adult models. High quality boots can hit double that base figure. Look for good, even, heavy stitching, a solid bond between upper and sole, and resistance to twisting motions such as you exert when turning skis.

If you are going to be skiing off the beaten track at all, you will also want a snow cuff. This is a padded area around the opening in the boot and will fit snugly against your ankle to keep snow from getting into the boot. All cross-country ski boots have three small holes drilled into the bottom to mate with the three pegs in cross-country ski bindings. Almost all manufacturers have adopted the Nordic norm to standardize the fit of boots to bindings, but it is still wise to actually try out your equipment for fit in the ski shop.

You may be surprised to see that many cross-country boots are lined only with a thin layer of leather-like street shoes. While your feet would freeze solid if you just stood around in them, the constant motion of skiing sends a steady flow of heat to the extremities. If you plan to tour during very cold weather and to stop for lunches, or if you suffer from cold feet, consider a pair of fleece-lined boots with room for a heavy pair of socks. You can beef up this insulation on very cold days by slipping another pair of heavy, wool socks right over your boots and lower legs.

Bindings

For most cross-country skiers there is only one type of binding, the toe clamp, sometimes called the rat-trap because of its shape. This light, inexpensive (about ten dollars) combination of aluminum plate and wire holds the sturdily built toe of a boot to the ski while leaving the heel completely free to rise and fall. This allows the skier to lunge forward over one ski at a time, thus shooting the ski across the snow.

The traditional toe clamp binding has a wire bail which snaps over the welt of the boot, but some new models are using variations on the design to allow pole-tip opening of the bindings and even step-in, self-locking catches. The heel plate is a simple metal and plastic affair with sawteeth to grip the boot heel. This gives some stability while making turns.

Persons bent on skiing in heavy bush and deep snow most of the time might consider the more constraining, but more stable heel clamp binding. This type of attachment was commonly used for skiing earlier in the century. Another type of cable binding has the locking clamp mounted in front of the toe piece.

By their nature, cable bindings restrict the lift of a skier's heel and do not allow the long, free strides which characterize true cross-country skiing. However, the moderately stiff cables give a skier far more control in turning skis and this is more important in mountain skiing and some deep snow situations in heavy bush.

Poles

While changes in technique in recent years dictated that downhill ski poles become shorter and relatively stiff, cross-country poles remain as long, flexible wands. They must have some spring to help catapult you forward with every stride, but also be strong enough to resist breaking when you lean on them for stability or even fall on them. The tips are curved rather than straight to make it easier to pull them from the snow as you move forward and the grips are slim and smooth to allow movement of your hand as you reach forward, then let the pole trail behind for a second. When buying poles make certain the straps are adjustable, since you will want to fit them snugly to whatever type of glove or mitt you are wearing.

For many years Tonkin bamboo was the standard material and it is still used for the cheapest poles. However, it has one serious disadvantage for the skier who will be making wilderness or downhill trips: it can break if you fall on it. Not only that, it can shatter into sharp splinters. At prices under ten dollars, a pair of Tonkin poles are good for beginners or skiers on a tight budget. But many consider it a good investment to double that outlay for the security of fiberglass or aluminium. If these are made of high-quality material, they are almost unbreakable.

Clothing

If three words can describe the right type of clothing for cross-country skiing they are, *light, loose and warm.* It is amazing how much heat the body can generate during the steady movements of skiing and how little clothing one can support even during cold weather. However, once you stop moving (for example, during a lunch break) the body quickly cools and will chill unless you have extra clothing at hand.

A basic outfit should include:

– A set of long underwear. Thermal designs, with a layer of cotton sewn to one of wool, have made the reputation of Duofold with both cross-country and downhill skiers. Be aware that this type of underwear is available in different weights for different climates. An alternative used by many is the fishnet-style underwear associated with Nordic countries. It allows for evaporation of sweat but does not give the wind protection of Duofold under severe conditions.

– A cotton turtleneck is next. There are many brands on the market but one of the most reliable over the years is the Medico. The turtleneck keeps your neck warm and allows evaporation of perspiration.

– Now slide on a pair of knee-length knicker socks. They should have some elasticity and should be long enough to prevent any cold gaps where the pants end. Some skiers like two pair of socks during cold conditions or like to use fleeced cotton "thermal" socks. However, wool is the best material for retaining warmth while wet.

– The knicker pants come next. Here the choice is wide, with everything from the once-popular corduroys, the poplin, cotton and nylon combinations, to the stretch knickers which cling to the body. Basically a hard, smooth, windproof but not waterproof material is best. Look for snug fitting cuffs and strong zippers in the pockets.

– On top goes a wool sweater, preferably of the flat knit type. This heavy material is quite wind-resistant and will shed snow better than the open knit styles. Hundreds of styles are available since this is the type of sweater used for years by downhill skiers. This sweater will run in the thirty dollars and over category, but it will keep you warm for years, probably decades.

– Last of the basic layers is the jacket, possibly part of a suit bought with the knickers. For light and general touring most skiers are using jackets made of the cotton, poplin or stretch nylon materials. They should have good ventilation but may feature a windproof panel in the front to keep your chest warm while allowing sweat to evaporate from behind.

– If you are not easily chilled you will enjoy the freedom of movement provided by ski gloves. During warm weather you can get by with a pair so light they look like driving or dress gloves. When the temperatures dip, you will need one of the thermal styles used by downhill skiers. If you suffer from cold hands most of the time, buy a pair of lined mitts, even down-filled ones if you really feel the cold.

– To cap it off you need a toque of the same type of wool as your sweater. Again those who suffer from the cold should look for the balaclava types which unfold to make a complete face mask. Some persons are very sensitive to cold wind in their ears. They should look for the windproof bonnets which will completely protect their heads or wear a jacket with a comfortable hood.

This basic outfit is all you need for an outing in all but severe weather, and during the spring you may well shed the jacket while in the sun. From here on you get into the extras that are useful and sometimes necessary. An insulated ski jacket is a handy piece of clothing for anyone, even a non-skier, and most people have one around the house. The most useful though no longer the most fashionable type is the "instructor" model which covers the hips and snugs against drafts with a belt.

Two types of linings are popular and both have their strong and weak points. Down is the classic for minimum weight and maximum insulation. It is expensive but in high demand for cold weather clothing and sleeping bags. There is one major disadvantage, however: when wet it compacts into a sodden mass with the insulation power of a used Kleenex. Wetness is not a common problem during the winter, but can occur during long expeditions or in spring conditions.

Synthetics, on the other hand, do not have quite the warmth of down but are generally cheaper and more resistant to compacting while wet. Mountaineers use both. If you are on a budget the choice is simple: synthetic. With a bit more money you should consider both carefully and ask the opinion of qualified people familiar with skiing conditions in your area.

A ski jacket may be a necessity if you are out on bitterly cold days and will almost certainly be one if you are planning overnight trips or even lunch breaks during cold weather. Lightweight down jackets, known as down sweaters, are useful for short trips when the weather looks as if it might turn cold and they are handy for lunch stops. Down is easily compacted, so these sweaters can be stuffed into a waterproof bag and will take up no more room than a loaf of bread.

Gaiters are a relatively new item in North America, but many skiers consider them essential for trips through deep snow. They are tubes of nylon or cotton which snug around your boot tops and reach to your calves. Gaiters keep snow from getting into your boots or sticking to your socks when you are travelling off the beaten track. During wet, spring conditions many skiers also use soft, neoprene boot covers which slip over their footwear like loose rubbers and prevent water from soaking the leather.

Wind or warm-up pants, which zipper completely open down the sides, became popular with downhill skiers during the mid-1960s. Though they are not necessary for most cross-country skiing, they can give needed insulation for someone spending a night camping out or travelling over exposed terrain during cold, windy weather.

When buying ski clothing there are a couple of points to watch. Cross-country skiing generates considerable perspiration, so you don't want clothing which is waterproofed because it will turn you into a perambulating sauna. When you stop moving, you will then become an ice cube. This rules out coated nylon except for specific cases where you expect to hit wet weather and need to keep clothing, especially down jackets, from getting wet.

There is a great range of styles and prices in ski clothing these days. Take your time to find something suited to your real needs and check for at least reasonable quality of construction. These days a lot of the European name brand manufacturers are having second line clothing made in the Far East from their last year's designs. This can provide well-styled gear with quite good quality at respectable savings.

In all cases, check the clothing for well-stitched seams and strong zippers and reject anything which does not look and feel sturdy.

Accessories

A skier in a big hurry, racing perhaps, might start out with no more than the skis beneath him and the skimpy racing suit on his back. However, most people out for a relaxed tour find they are in need of such odds and ends as fresh or different wax, a Kleenex, some suntan lotion or a snack on the last leg home. Over the years most people build up some sort of casual checklist of things to stuff in pockets or pouch before each trip.

The essentials for most skiers start with a pack of at least two or three waxes, a scraper to remove old wax and a cork to smooth on a new coat. Even if you are just wandering through a woodlot, it can be useful to refer to a compass for the quickest route back to the car and in wilderness skiing a compass is *essential*. Under the sun, dark glasses are useful to prevent eyestrain and during cloudy, windy or snowy conditions, yellow goggles make the going a lot easier. Both types

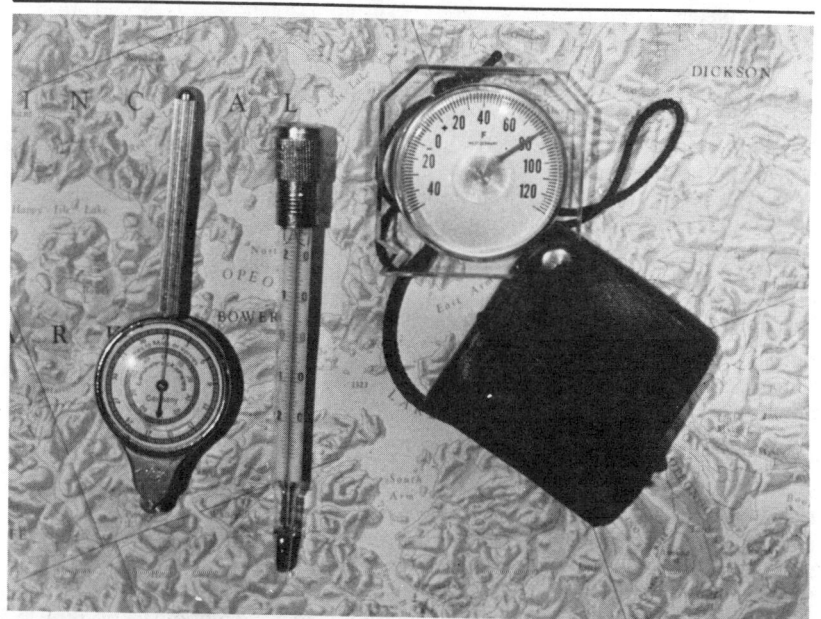

Three useful little items for the touring skier: a measuring instrument for maps, snow thermometer to help in choosing wax and a pocket thermometer.

Fanny pack with some equipment for a short trip. Included are: wax kit, cork and scraper, spare ski tip, snow thermometer, waterproof match case, knife, compass and suntan lotion.

of eye protection keep those eye pokers, twigs, from jabbing you while you are in bush country.

By now you have probably filled your pockets with the little essentials for any outing on skis. But if you are roaming off the beaten track or on a long trail in a resort, you may want a few more extras. It is probably easiest to get a pouch belt commonly called a fanny pack and stow in it the most regularly used items along with a bit of emergency gear.

This would include a spare ski tip (preferably the metal kind) for any lengthy trips, matches in a waterproof metal container sold in sporting goods stores, a stout folding knife or a hunting knife in a solid sheath, a hank of orange parachute cord also sold in sporting goods stores and a couple of chocolate bars and some Dextrose tablets. In addition, it is wise to carry a map of the area if possible or even sketch one out on a piece of paper if you can get details of the trail before starting out.

The list can keep growing if you are planning a trip in real wilderness, where an emergency could force you to make an emergency camp. In this case you should carry a small packsack with suitable equipment. This will be discussed in detail in the chapter on touring and winter camping.

Quality

Everybody loves a bargain and with a sport as popular as cross-country skiing, there is lots of competition and considerable choice. Many of the Nordic manufacturers have been in the business for generations and their names are a guarantee of quality. Many of the newcomers to the business are using modern technology to produce equipment even stronger than the best handmade product. However, the old saying that you get what you pay for applies to some degree even in this sport.

Under the forty dollar range, the skis tend to lack the sophistication and sturdy construction of more expensive equipment. Cheaper boots may start off well, but they tend to split and rot at the seams before their more expensive counterparts do. Poles that are too cheap won't last as long. Bindings that are too fragile will bend or break, clothing ill-woven and poorly sewn will rip and tear at awkward times.

All this is relative of course. Cheap equipment will function very well for the casual skier who wants only the occasional tour around a nearby trail, but it might fail under the heavy stress of a long trip through the heavy snows of wilderness skiing. The rule is to match quality to the type of skiing you expect to do and never to buy something that looks in the shop as if it will jam, bend or break, because on the trail it surely will. Hans Gmoser, the Austrian mountaineer who founded helicopter skiing in Western Canada and made it world famous, writes to all skiers planning to tackle the difficult mountain conditions: "In the mountains, the best is only just good enough and repairs are difficult to make in remote places such as these."

Basic Technique

One of the commonest phrases used to describe the simplicity of this sport is: "If you can walk, you can cross-country ski." Some skiing parents find that their children are able to slide around on skis even before they can walk across the living room floor. This is not surprising considering the extra stability of a pair of skis. Once you get used to the feel of the boards under your feet and make the mandatory few falls which await any beginner, you will find the skis stable on level ground and quite manageable on gentle slopes.

Over the past 4,000 or so years people have tried skis ranging from a few feet to more than nine feet in length and have even used two skis of different lengths. For most of that period they resorted to a single pole, usually about six feet long and sharpened at one end. This produced a technique not unlike that of a canoeist or rafter poling his way down a stream. In the past century things have been sorted out into a simple, natural form which is basically a step and glide using a pair of matched poles for stability, rhythm and propulsion.

While downhill skiing involves complicated manoeuvres of weight shifting, body twisting and knee bending to accomplish competent (let alone graceful) descents, cross-country skiing is relatively simple. A skier usually needs several years to become reasonably proficient in downhill technique but only a single season, with lessons, to be fully at ease on cross-country equipment.

Lessons are highly recommended, especially by those skiers who have learned the hard way trying to teach themselves. A few dollars invested in professional instruction saves many hours of trial and error. To begin with, there is a trained skier calling out the learning steps as you need them and setting a proper pace in a good learning area. Just as important, the instructor can detect errors in technique that you can't see in yourself at an early stage and that can be eliminated before they become ingrained as bad habits.

This series of photographs illustrates the basic learning sequence for someone starting the sport. It shows the progression from walking on skis to the diagonal stride, the name given to the technique used for cross-country motion. Next displayed are simple methods of climbing and skiing down hills under control. The demonstration is provided by John Ardill, director of cross-country skiing at Seneca College of Applied Arts and Technology, just north of Toronto. This is the technique generally used by cross-country ski instructors across Canada.

Starting Off

Two of the first things a beginner should learn before setting out on his first trip are how to set a proper track and a proper pace. Though it may seem too simple to discuss, the laying of a good track in fresh snow is obviously not understood by many skiers. Witness the wandering ruts that result when someone leading the way doesn't keep their skis evenly apart. Once such a track has been used a couple of times, the compacted snow freezes and everyone who follows is stuck with a trail on which they cannot get a smooth, even glide. The lead skier should keep his skis consistently about a handsbreadth apart and keep a sharp eye peeled ahead for obstacles so he can make gentle, even curves in the track, which will not slow following skiers.

Pace is important for any skier, very important when there is a group and crucial in wilderness or mountain skiing. A person in even moderately good physical condition can easily ski a half day on flat land if he follows a steady pace which will not wear him out in the first hour or so. Even racers who are moving fast are actually keeping themselves in control to save some energy for the last leg of the trail.

On a group trip of more than a couple of hours duration, the leader should keep a sharp eye on the party to make sure the pace is not too fast for the weakest member. He should set a pace which will allow a good, smooth diagonal stride but which will not tire anyone too quickly. If the party is breaking trail through new snow it is a good idea to rotate the leadership so that one person will not become exhausted with this chore.

As in any sport there are some simple rules of etiquette. It is the responsibility of the skier coming from behind, be it on a flat track or going downhill, to avoid persons in front and to warn them of his approach with the shout: "track," and more usefully, "track on your right" or "track on your left." The skier ahead on a trail should avoid any sudden moves and should step aside as much as possible so the person behind can pass.

When you fall in soft snow you will create a hole known among skiers as a *sitzmark*. Particularly on a trail or well-used slope, it is important to fill in such a crater so it won't trip the next skier. If you are climbing a slope, avoid hacking up the track used by skiers coming down the hill.

Advanced Skiing

After you have a good grasp of the fundamentals and feel at ease gliding along a smooth track or snowplowing down gentle hills, you may be interested in developing a more professional style. For the diagonal stride, that means perfecting all the little movements which go into the technique. These include working on the evenness of your stride, eliminating any tendency to rock from side to side, planting your poles at the right angle, relaxing your grip on them as you finish the push and getting the most from each glide. The best person to help you polish your technique and get the most from each movement is a good instructor. In addition, you can learn a lot from watching racers and other professional skiers who have worked for years to develop an almost serpentine smoothness and power in their movements. Avoid paying too much attention to other skiers learning the sport, since you can easily pick up bad habits as well as good ones from them.

Skiing downhill, whether on the heavy equipment specifically designed for that sport or on the light, cross-country equipment, is where the techniques of skiing finally meet again. This is not to suggest that you should tackle the steep, hard packed slopes of Mt. Tremblant or Mt. Norquay on cross-country equipment. With the soft boots and flexible bindings which allow an easy stride, you lack the turning power which comes with heavy equipment and without steel edges, you would probably slide half way down the hill before grinding to a halt.

But a snowplow is a snowplow on any pair of skis and this applies even for christies, in which the skis are kept parallel throughout the turn. Most people can make snowplow turns on cross-country skis on snow that is not too hard packed and good skiers can make linked christies down mountain slopes which are not too steep and have soft, fluffy snow. In fact, out on the trail anything goes if it helps you get down the hill more efficiently. The famous Herman "Jack Rabbit" Smith-Johannsen once astounded a companion when they were skiing a steep slope through the trees by lowering himself through the brush by hanging onto branches and letting them slide through his grasp.

Walking
Ignoring your ski poles at first, you can get the feeling of the skis by simply walking forward in a straight line on smooth, level snow, letting your arms swing freely. The aim is to develop a relaxed stride and there is no attempt to slide the skis at this stage.

Forward Shuffle
Here you begin to get the feel of sliding. You flex your knees and, using the same track in the snow as before, literally shuffle along, taking short glides as you step briskly forward onto one ski after the other.

Kick and Glide
This movement is the basis of good cross-country ski technique. Starting on your track in the snow, bend your knees, advance one ski slightly and put most of your weight on it. Then slide the rear ski forward, stepping onto this ski as it moves in front of you. As you step forward, push yourself ahead by kicking backward with the other foot. For a moment, the trailing ski will have no weight on it, as shown in the photo above. This kicking motion will propel you into a glide along the track, giving the first sensation of cross-country skiing.

Double Poling: Push
Now leave the kicking for a time and take up your poles to learn the second half of your propulsion technique. Plant the tips of the poles a few inches in front of and to each side of the bindings. The poles should be slightly angled to the rear. Bend your knees and pull yourself forward. As your hands pass your hips, bend forward at the waist and push as you slide past the poles.

Double Poling: Finish
Keep bending forward at the waist to get the last ounce of push into a glide, then let the poles trail out behind you, relaxing your grip on the handles a bit. On a hard, fast track or while going down a gentle hill, double poling alone will increase your speed.

Diagonal Stride
This is what cross-country skiing really looks like. It is the motion which can propel a skier over fifty miles or more of terrain in a day. The diagonal stride combines all the techniques previously learned, using the swinging arm you began with – except that now you are pulling, then pushing on a pole with each swing. In fact, the rhythm of the arms sets the pace for the legs and determines how fast or slow you will ski at any given time.

Uphill Diagonal Stride
As the steepness of the slope increases, the stride becomes shorter, the knees are bent more and there is more of a springing motion. There has to be a definite weight shift to plant each ski and make the waxed base adhere to the snow. At times you will literally stamp your skis into the snow to make them stick on a steep climb. Also, you will lean harder on your poles and they will serve as brakes if you start to slide backward.

Double Poling with Kick
This is a combination of the kick and glide, and double poling techniques. In addition to a push with both poles, you give a kick with first one leg, then the other; but instead of gliding on one ski, as in the diagonal stride, you glide on both as in the original double pole method. This is useful for increasing your speed on flat ground or on a gentle downgrade, and gives you a bit more speed than the simple double poling.

Herringbone
When the slope gets too steep for a straight climb and your skis are constantly slipping, spread the tips apart as much as necessary to regain traction. You will be taking short steps and planting the poles behind the skis but will keep moving at a reasonable speed.

Sidestepping
This is the slow but sure method to make your way up or down virtually any slope. Simply turn your skis at right angles to the hill, bend your hips, knees and ankles into the hill if necessary to get more bite into the snow from the edges of your skis and begin stepping your way up the hill.

Downhill Traverse
As the old saying has it, what goes up must come down. You could sidestep back down the hill or if things get desperate take off your skis and walk down. There's no shame in that. However, it's much more exhilarating to start running straight down small hills, if there's lots of room at the bottom and then to tackle bigger hills. Here the skier is traversing across the slope at an angle to keep his speed down. He is bent slightly at the waist, knees and ankles, has more than half his weight on his downhill ski, has advanced the tip of his uphill ski and has angled his hips slightly into the hill.

Snowplow
This is the basic method for slowing, stopping or turning on skis. Coming down the hill you keep the ski tips together, tails apart (opposite of the herringbone climb) and press your knees toward the ski tips to increase the bite of your ski edges. It is a simple and very useful manoeuvre.

Snowplow Turn

This fundamental turn begins with the snowplow. Plant your heels firmly on the serrated plates to get a good grip, press forward with your knees and twist your feet to apply steering action. As you turn you will place more weight on the downhill ski. By alternating the movements you can make a series of linked turns down a long hill, keeping your speed under control and avoiding obstacles.

Waxing

Waxing is one of those subjects which looks terribly complicated on paper but is not very hard once you have the stuff in your hands. The making of ski wax has been compared to a black art and the bubbling concoctions in some mixing pots furthers that impression. Nineteenth century residents of the United States west used to amuse themselves during the winter by racing on skis they had dubbed "Norwegian snowshoes". The racers would "dope" the bases of their seven to twelve-foot long skis with imaginative mixtures of pitch, tar, tallow, castor oil, rosin and other ingredients. The results were impressive: these human missiles could hit speeds up to 90 mph.

Modern ski waxes may still contain a few trade secrets and they are also intended to be as easy as possible to apply. Many manufacturers are producing two-wax kits: one for dry snow and the other for wet conditions. In Canada one of the best known of these is the Jack Rabbit wax kit.

First a bit of theory to explain why waxing is needed. For many years skiers relied on the natural friction of wood on snow for the grip needed to get moving. In deep snow this worked not too badly, but on any smooth surface there was obviously a lot of backsliding. Then one day an anonymous but inspired skier discovered that wax has a natural propensity to stick to snow along with a lot of other things. From there on it was just a matter of time to find a series of waxes of different hardness which would not only stick to snow when skis were stationary and weighted, but that would slide easily once they got moving.

There is a lot of chemistry and physics involved, but essentially tiny snow crystals will grip a waxed surface much as sand would. When a skier lifts a waxed ski and slides it forward, this grip is broken and the friction of the moving ski will momentarily melt the snow beneath and the ski will be riding on a minute layer of water. As soon as the ski stops, the snow crystallizes and the tiny bits of ice grip the wax. This is why a well-used ski trail or slope becomes icy with continued use.

The secret in getting both a good grip and glide is in matching the hardness of the wax to the hardness of the snow. This can be done by squeezing a handful of snow to see if it stays dry and fluffy, indicating considerable cold and a hard wax; if it compacts, indicating a medium wax; or drips water, indicating a soft wax. For greater precision, measure snow temperature with a thermometer and refer to the instructions on wax packages.

The easiest way to begin is with a package of two or three waxes, which will handle most snow conditions. With experience you will probably add a few more waxes and one or two of the sticky klister waxes used for very icy or very wet runs. Most skiers like to pick up a rectangular waxing cork to get the thin, smooth, hard layer of wax suitable for dry snow conditions. However wax can be easily applied

In a pinch you can use the palm of your hand to rub wax onto a ski. Note how dabs of klister have been applied, ready to be rubbed smooth along the ski base.

and rubbed in with the palm of your hand. A scraper is a handy item for removing old wax or the wrong kind of wax.

When you are starting out it is best to put on a wax which is too hard rather than too soft. A softer wax can always be rubbed on over a harder wax but the reverse is not true. As well, a harder wax will give you greater speed and if you are slipping a bit you might get by just rubbing a rough "kicker strip" of the next softest wax on the centre one-third of your ski bases. If there are at least two skiers you don't even need to take off your skis for this.

A few more tips in what is really a brief survey of the subject: wax your skis indoors, then set them outside to cool for at least a half hour if possible and "run-in" the wax for a couple of minutes before deciding to try another hardness if you are not moving smoothly. If you have just bought a new pair of wood skis, the salesman should have explained the necessity for pine-tarring the bases to seal them against water and therefore warping. Many shops will do the job for a nominal charge, but if you enjoy messing around a bit, tarring your own skis can give you a better feeling for the sport.

There are two methods: cold tar and hot tar. The cold tar is simply brushed on from the can and then rubbed in with a cloth. It is a relatively simple procedure but does not penetrate the wood as well as the hot tar, which is brushed on and then gently heated with a blowtorch until it bubbles a bit. In either case, only apply a thin coat of tar and the bases should be slightly tacky when they have cooled. Of course with the synthetic bases tarring is unnecessary, but you usually need to apply a special coat of binding wax to provide a good grip for the various waxes you will use on the trail.

This is an outline of the subject of waxing. More detailed information is available in other books or magazines and in brochures distributed free by many wax companies.

Conditioning
Cross-country skiing can be one of the most physically demanding sports in the world. Studies of racers have shown they burn as many as 2,500 calories per hour– more than competition swimmers or marathon runners. Most of the skier's body is in almost constant motion: the arms are pulling, then pushing on the poles, the legs are flexing, the torso is twisting and the feet are springing. After about one-half hour of fast skiing the body will have exhausted its ready supply of carbohydrates, in the form of glycogen, and will begin to burn its reserves of fat. This is why serious cross-country skiers are slim and wiry.

Cross-country skiing is undoubtedly one of the best physical conditioners, especially since it can be pursued at your own pace. As with any sport, you should already be at least in reasonable physical shape before starting serious activity. This is particularly important for anyone who knows or suspects they may be prone to a heart problem. But even the young, apparently healthy person who drives to work and to the corner store for a pack of cigarettes and considers a dip in the pool his exercise should make some preparation for skiing.

One of the best ways to get in good physical shape and stay that way is to find several sports or activities which will carry you through the changing seasons. For example, you may swim and play tennis during the summer, cycle whenever the roads are free from snow, canoe, hike, climb mountains, play squash or soccer to name just a few of the many sports. Even walking and especially jogging and running are good conditioners which will help get your legs and lungs in shape for skiing.

If this is your first time on skis remember the old saying: easy does it at first. There is a good, medical reason for this. If you push your muscles well beyond their normal levels of activity, you will trigger several chemical processes including the buildup of lactate, a combustion product of overexertion. The result, in simple terms, is muscle stiffness, which can leave you with all the suppleness of a mannequin for the next couple of days.

If you feel "out of shape" before you take to the trails, try to work in at least a few brisk walks and some light calisthenics for at least a week or two before putting on the skis. Then start with a lesson and a half day of skiing and take the rest of the day to relax and enjoy the scenery. You'll feel a lot better for it and be in better shape for the next day.

Touring and Winter Camping

Touring

If you have learned the basic technique of cross-country skiing, have skied a few trails at resorts and are enthusiastic for new adventures, you are ready for touring. Touring takes you beyond the simple outing on a short trail. There is no hard and fast line between the two, but basically the touring skier is heading out for at least a day on the trails and often plans a trip of several days duration. If one thing physically separates him from the non-touring skier, it is the pack on his back—in which he carries food and drink, plus other equipment to meet any emergencies encountered on the trip.

In Europe, especially in Scandinavia and around the Alps, ski touring has been popular for decades and there are many well established trails leading from one cabin or hotel to another, allowing days of potential travel on one trip. There you find people of all ages. Youth groups, school classes, friends and families take winter holidays to seek out fresh snow and sunshine and escape the gloom of winter in the cities.

North Americans are just starting to catch up with the Europeans. In the New England states it is possible to ski from one hotel to another for several days and have a room and hot bath waiting each night. During the 1930s Jack Rabbit Johannsen laid out the Maple Leaf Trail in the Laurentians, north of Montreal. It ran from Labelle for 80 miles south to Shawbridge and Johannsen was canny enough to lay it between hotels so he could always find a place to stay at night. In the Rockies, alpine clubs have used well established cabins as way stations on ski tours, but these were placed for trips in which climbing mountains to ski down untracked snow was the aim.

Where should one look for touring trails?

Most of Canada can be toured during the winter, but it is wise to start out at least on terrain that is not too rugged or bushy. You don't want an expedition to lay new trails; you want to enjoy skiing paths that already exist. Obviously you will avoid rocky terrain at the start of the season when the snow cover is light and will keep away from marshes and watercourses during thaws. Flatland is ideal for keeping up your speed, but it can get boring so that you will soon be looking for rolling countryside. If it is a windy day, you will seek trails through the woods rather than in open fields and if you are competent on the downhill pitches, you will seek out and enjoy a few runs down gentle hills. Just make sure everyone in your party is as capable as the leader.

There are three main sources of prepared trails and the condition of their routes will range from barely cleared and marked to carefully mapped and groomed each day. First is the commercial operation– a ski resort, lodge or hotel. This is a profit-making venture, so there will be a fee, usually a dollar or two for a day of skiing, or it may be included in the cost of your accommodation. Commercial trails tend to be loops of a few miles in length, though some have pushed out wilderness trails allowing scope for even the winter camper who wants at least a two-day run. Commercial trails are usually well marked and are often groomed.

Then there are ski club trails, usually laid across public or private land with the consent of the owner. These are generally "free" in the sense that there is no one sitting at the entrance to charge you a fee, but the clubs try to finance the operation by selling memberships and possibly trail maps. Since the marking and maintenance of the trails is a voluntary operation, it is often wise to invest in a map and possibly key it to a topographic map for the area to aid you in navigation. Club trails may wander for a mile or two through some farm fields or they may penetrate mountain valleys and northern forests for many miles. There are even efforts to link up trails as in the North Shore area of Quebec. In addition to trail information, club membership introduces one to people with similar interests and often provides free or discounted lessons, equipment clinics, travel and expertise on the sport.

The third type of organized ski trail is found on parkland: federal, provincial and municipal. Many governments are just starting to respond to the demand for more ski trails, so the availability of such routes tends to be spotty. Some are professionally maintained and there is even a service charge. Others, including some done under such auspices as the now defunct Local Initiatives Program, have been blazed but are no longer maintained.

Many of the national parks, especially those in the west, have developed trails; a large number of provincial parks are creating trails and some cities have even laid out trails within their boundaries. Beyond these organized routes there is an endless expanse of countryside, much of it laced with paths of one form or another which can be skied. Hiking trails are an obvious choice, but you should check them out before planning a day trip along one of these. Remember that hikers don't have to manoeuvre on skis, so the trail may twist through heavy brush or include a number of steep sections on rocky hillsides. Most trail clubs can supply you with maps and information about the suitability of various sections of their footpaths for skiing.

Canoe routes are another definite possibility, especially for canoeists who enjoyed the countryside during the summer and would like to see it again during the winter. Again a couple of things to watch out for. Portage trails are cleared for use during the summer and if there is several feet of snow on the ground you may find your head in the branches, slowing your pace in some sections. Also, a well-worn footpath is easy to follow in the summer but may not be so obvious in the winter when everything is beneath a smooth blanket of snow. Of course, the route is largely over water, so you must be on the lookout for any potential hazards.

Then there are unplowed rural roads and bush tracks such as fire roads and logging roads where you can lay your own track. You are limited only by your imagination and the stock of maps you lay in.

About the only type of track to avoid if possible is the well-used snowmobile trail, and this may not always be easy. One or two passes of a snowmobile are fine for compacting fresh snow and making it a lot easier to ski, but a regularly used machine trail quickly becomes full of undulations. In addition, you will be bothered by their noise and the fact you will have to get off the track frequently.

Even as this book is being written, resort operators are expanding their ski trails, hoteliers are realizing the scope of the ski boom and are laying out trail networks from their front doors and ski club members, armed with saws and surveyor's tape, are marking new routes through the countryside. All this augurs well for the touring skier; there are ever more trails for trips of a day, a week or a month.

Many Canadians are starting to realize this and are quietly booking their vacations during the winter, when it is easy to get time off from most jobs, and are heading away to a favorite lodge in the north country. There, they and their families spend day after day exploring the silent countryside as they never could in summer. Evenings are spent in camaraderie around a roaring fireplace or in a quiet corner with a book or some topographical maps. At night, the tired skiers crawl under heavy, wool blankets, down sleeping bags for a well-earned rest.

The step into touring should be a natural one from short trips. If you are leaving well-travelled terrain it should be in a party of three or more skiers. Travelling alone in wild country can be exhilarating but it also brings risks which you should regard seriously. If you have an accident, even a simple one, you must be prepared to make your way back out alone through deep snow and cold and without any help. This is exhilarating only if you succeed.

Better to have at least one skier to stay with you while another goes for help. No matter how large the party, you should leave word with some responsible person just where you are going and when you expect to return. If you don't show up after a reasonable length of time, there will be someone near a phone to call for help. As a minimum measure, you should leave a note inside the windshield of your car indicating where you are going and when you expect to return. In the national parks of western Canada, where conditions can be hazardous at times, touring skiers are required to register when they leave for a trip and to check back in when they return.

For even a half day on a little used trail, you should carry a fanny pack with a few emergency items as listed in the accessories section. If you are heading out for a day in the wilderness, you should carry more.

What is wilderness skiing? Mike Exall, the outdoor recreation co-ordinator for Seneca College, provides this definition: "You are in wilderness when you get into areas no longer bounded by concession roads." In such an area it is possible to become lost and get into serious trouble if you are not prepared to navigate and, if necessary, make an emergency camp.

For many years mountain guides, many of them from European alpine centres, have been leading climbers and skiers into the mountains of Western Canada. These guides must be expert at coping with the terrain, making regular or emergency camps, finding their way through adverse conditions and coping with emergencies such as avalanches, rockfalls or injuries in a party.

The Canadian Ski Association (CSA) recognized that the boom in cross-country skiing was creating a similar need for guides who could lead skiers across non-mountainous terrain. Exall, a mountaineer, skier and outdoor instructor with experience in Europe, New Zealand and Canada, prepared the manual for training such leaders. He feels anyone who takes a tour of any size into the back country should be trained in such things as tour preparation, the psychology of leading a group, navigation, survival, first aid, rescue and evacuation. Graduates of the CSA courses can be identified by oblong pins bearing the title "Cross-country Tour Leader" over a maple leaf. This pin is an assurance that the wearer has been trained to safely guide parties through wilderness conditions in everything but the high country.

There are three levels of certification. The lowest level, indicated by a bronze pin, denotes a leader qualified to take skiers on day tours or overnight tours if the party is making its way to some permanent shelter such as a cabin. The silver pin goes to leaders qualified to handle any type of winter tour, including winter camping trips which will involve tenting out. A gold pin is worn by leaders who are also qualified to examine candidates for the other two levels.

Ski parties have been heading into the wilderness for many years without the benefit of certified leaders and will obviously continue to do so for many more years. However, in the past, the kind of person adventurous enough to tackle the winter wilderness was usually someone already oriented to and experienced in outdoors living. Over the years he had picked up some expertise by reading and being with other outdoorsmen and had earned a healthy respect for the wild country.

Now tens of thousands of people, many of them permanent city dwellers, are taking up the sport of cross-country skiing and after learning the basics, will be looking for new fields and forests to conquer. Naturally many of them will want to try some of the trails of our provincial and national parks, logging roads through forest land, wilderness hiking and even animal trails.

Anyone who wants to tour off the beaten track would be well advised to start this kind of tripping with other skiers experienced in such travel. If you don't know any personally, you can probably find them in one of the many ski clubs. There is no better way to learn than by watching someone who already knows how it is done.

Before setting out on day-long tours, you should try a few half-day trips to get the feel of breaking trail through fresh snow and to gauge your own ability to handle the rigors of such travel. This will also give you some experience in simple navigation; for example, learning how to decide which fork of a trail takes you in the direction you want to go.

You should have three things prepared in advance of any tour. First, you need to know where you are going and how you are going to find your way—in precise terms. This means a knowledge of the trail marking system if there is one, a map of the area if it is not very well marked or you suspect it may not be clear at points, a compass and the ability to use it. Secondly, you need the knowledge and preferably some training on how to cope with possible emergencies ranging from a broken ski tip to a broken leg. Thirdly, you need the proper equipment.

The ski tourer is easily distinguished by a packsack carrying food, extra clothing and equipment to cope with any problems which might arise. A good packsack is a small mountaineer's type bag made of waterproof nylon and having well padded and easily adjustable shoulder straps and a waist strap to keep it from flopping from side to side and throwing you off balance. Make sure you get a decent sized bag so you can stuff in adequate supplies of food, drink and bulky, but warm clothing to wear during lunch breaks or if the weather turns foul. Look for such features as side pockets to carry small items you may want in a hurry, such as wax, a map pocket in the flap and loops or other means of attaching your skis if you want to carry them a short distance. There are many good sacks on the market, starting at about twenty-five dollars, and the best way to find a good one is to ask other skiers what they like and check out a couple of good outdoor stores.

Here is a suggested list of what you might put in the bag for a day tour:
wax kit, including cork and scraper
spare ski tip
sunglasses and yellow goggles
nylon cord
map and compass
sheath knife or heavy folding knife
hatchet (unless you will be above the timberline)
repair kit with tape, wire, binding screws, screwdriver and tool to make holes in skis
matches in waterproof container
plastic garbage bags
first aid kit
food and drink for a hearty lunch plus emergency rations
warm jacket plus waterproof clothing if rain is a possibility
flashlight
tarpaulin: heavy plastic, coated nylon or a "space blanket"
a metal cup or can for melting snow into drinking water
heavy mitts and extra socks
gaiters
wind pants (if you could hit severe weather)
fire starter– a heavy candle stub is useful.
Kleenex

Winter Camping

This is a sport which has developed across Canada along with cross-country skiing. Until recent years it was the domain of the hardy trapper, the Eskimo, the lonely Mountie on patrol, the mountaineer or the adventurer. It is still a sport for the hardy and vigorous and one area where there will never be crowded campsites.

There is a satisfaction in being very close to nature when she is in a tough mood. You down a meal before it can freeze on your plate, bed down with just a thin layer of material between you and the frigid elements and turn through the night to avoid freezing the part of your body in contact with the ground. There is a great satisfaction in awakening the next morning to make a hot cup of tea laced with honey and to stagger out of the tent to watch a sunrise over the frozen landscape.

Relatively few Canadians can say they have pitched a tent in the middle of winter, taken a last run across moonlit snow and listened to the cry of coyotes or the howl of a distant timberwolf as they dozed off. Obviously it is not the sort of adventure to be taken lightly. Everything must be organized and functioning properly or you will be in for a long, very cold night. Novices should not try such a trip unless they are with a seasoned winter camper who can check out their equipment, pitch camp and make meals. The best way to learn the skills, of course, is to start camping with someone who has done it many times. It is also possible to get training with a number of ski clubs and organizations such as community colleges. Naturally a person planning winter camping would be well advised to have summer camping experience to provide a grounding in the methods of tenting.

In addition to experience, good equipment is essential. If necessary, you can spend a night of reasonable comfort in a lean-to shelter with a roaring campfire in front—provided you have warm clothing and a thick sleeping bag. Once you stop moving and especially after the sun sets, you will need lots of insulation. A good combination is a heavy ski parka and insulated warm-up pants of the type worn by downhill skiers. Ski gloves will no longer be warm enough and you should opt for down-lined mitts or possibly the heavy wool mitts from Europe. A good combination is a pair of light gloves inside the mitts so you can tackle finicky jobs without exposing your hands.

The light ski boots are little insulation, even if you follow the standard advice and put on a fresh, dry pair of socks. Better to throw in a pair of insulated mukluks or lined snowmobile boots for knocking around camp. That way you'll be well covered from head to toe. If you start getting chilled you not only start fumbling simple tasks, your body and mind slow down.

You will need a good-sized pack to carry all the gear for a night out. While the frame packs so favored in the summer will carry the freight very nicely, they do not have a good balance for cross-country skiing, especially on downhill pitches. These high-riding packs tend to overbalance a skier and many a person has found himself buried face first in the snow as a result. A better choice, if you can afford it, is a mountain climber's sack designed to hug the body. However, these packs tend to run in the fifty dollar and over range.

In addition to the equipment already prepared for a day pack, you will need to add more food and clothing, more eating utensils and some specialized equipment. Most important is the sleeping bag. Here you can get into great discussions about material and design, but essentially you will need what is called a ''winter'' bag rated by the manufacturer for the lowest temperature you expect to encounter. This way you still have a safety margin in your ski jacket and overpants, which you can wear at night for extra insulation.

Every year more models of sleeping bags are coming on the market, so you will face a wide choice. It is virtually impossible to rent or try out new bags, so the best

The first job of any winter chef is melting snow for drinking water and cooking. This is a time and fuel consuming task.

way to shop is to talk first with experienced winter campers and see how the insulating loft of their bags stood up to usage. Loft is the term used to describe how much the insulating material will fluff up once the bag is unpacked. This creation of airspace between the feathers or synthetic fibres is what provides insulation. Unfortunately for your pocketbook, high quality materials and workmanship needed to design, fill and finish a good bag lead to price tags over $100. However, it is an investment which will last for a long time.

Fire for warmth and cooking is another major requirement. You can make a campfire if you have the time and energy to find and cut dry wood and haul it through the snow, but even then you may face the prospect of trying to keep a fire going and cook outside during a snowstorm. Most winter campers rely on a portable stove which can be used outside the tent, at the entrance or (with great caution and adequate ventilation) inside the tent if a storm is blowing. The use of such stoves is something which should be learned from experts since a wrong move can create a severe fire hazard and the loss of your shelter is a serious matter during the winter.

The Optimus 111B has been the standard stove for many years. It burns readily available white gas and has a pressure pump. Similar stoves without a pump or the bottled gas stoves so handy and so popular in the summer are not suitable for cold weather usage, since low temperatures drastically reduce the pressure inside the fuel tanks.

Shelter can take many forms. Eskimos have lived for millenia in igloos, Indians made do with simple wooden shelters and wilderness travellers have survived if not flourished, huddled under the thick, low branches of evergreens. Some winter

Full kit for winter camping. Included are mountain-style pack, winter tent, gas stove, cooking, first aid and repair equipment. In front are waterproof boot covers for wet travel conditions.

adventurers who are making a base camp on a long trip actually prefer to build a snow cave or igloo, especially if they have to wait out a severe storm.

Most winter campers who don't have a cabin at the end of the trail rely on tents. You can get by decently with many of the summer tents, especially if you are camping in forested areas sheltered from high winds. Some designs are more suitable than others for the rigors and problems of winter camping. For example, many of the new tents are self-supporting thanks to fiberglass rods which eliminate the need for burying guy ropes in the snow. Usually these models are highly wind resistant and with half-tunnel shapes provide a large amount of useable room inside. So-called mountain tents have such special features as poles which are braced on the tents themselves rather than on the ground, flaps around the edge so the tent can be banked with snow to prevent winds from sweeping underneath and snugly closing doors.

Check Lists

Most campers have their favorite stories, usually told in the third person, of things left behind on long trips. These can range from the silly and embarrassing (such as toilet paper) to the more serious (boots or stove). The best way to avoid adding your own story to the record is to create a personal checklist of all your own gear, ranging from the apparently obvious– skis– to such minutae as the contents of the toilet and medicine kit.

It is important to itemize everything down to the last piece of clothing for two reasons. The main problem we all face when heading out for a trip is simply forgetting something because we do not use it every day. This is more a problem for beginners but even experts have been known to rush out of the house without their ski boots. In addition it is a control on things that are used up or damaged during a trip and not replaced immediately. If you check everything against a list ahead of time you have a chance to repair or replace the item.

Following is the suggested list for an overnight pack but it should be treated only as a guide to each individual. You should create your own list around equipment you have or may need for particular trips.

basic contents of a day kit
change of underclothing
sleeping bag suitable for coldest weather likely
ensolite pad
mukluks or other warm boots for camp
water bottle (plastic or aluminium)
bowl, cup, spoon, fork and knife
sunburn cream
personal toilet kit with any medicines you need personally

In addition, there is gear which is needed by a party and would normally be distributed between members to equalize the weight and bulk. This would include:
tent
stove and fuel
shovel
one large, first aid kit
food, including survival rations
cooking pots and utensils
pot cleaning cloths, pads and paper towels
large, collapsible water jug

Eating Out

Food becomes a key part of any trip lasting anything more than half a day and during the winter it should be something hot (if possible) and nourishing. While the menu for a day trip can be relatively haphazard, and hopefully fun, longer trips require a bit more thought or else good instincts built up over years of experience. On a long trip the body is running on its natural reserves if they are not replenished in amounts at least equal to what has been burned. A balanced diet must include carbohydrates, proteins and fats totalling more than 4,300 calories a day. A good ration is about a kilogram (2.2 pounds) in dry weight of food per day and this will bulk out somewhat when water is added to make soups and stews. In addition, many wilderness travellers add a vitamin pill per day to their menu to cope with any deficiencies caused by the change from a home diet.

Actually, water is first on the list of priorities since one can survive several days without food but much less without water. Eating some snow will not drop you in your tracks as some fables have it, but eating a lot of snow to get a relatively small amount of liquid will chill and tire your body. (Snow, especially if it is light and powdery, is more air than ice.)

The best way to cope with the water siutation is to start off with a full metal or plastic bottle of water per person and when the container gets about half empty pack it tightly with the wettest, densest snow available. As that mixture sloshes around it will melt into water by the time you are ready for another drink. This system is not likely to keep up with your thirst however and at night it will be necessary to melt enough snow to refill all water bottles completely. Leave them between sleeping bags and they won't freeze. If you are in a large group it may be more convenient to fill a plastic half-gallon jug for the night.

Naturally you will look first for unpolluted running water. Even in the winter there are a suprising number of spring-fed streams which remain open, though some have to be located by digging through several feet of snow and chopping a bit of ice. Just be extra careful not to fall in. Instead try dipping from a distance with a cooking pot tied to the end of a ski pole and rope yourself with climbing rope or nylon parachute cord before clambering down steep river banks.

Next in priority is the so-called survival food. This can range from the classic chocolate bar stuffed in a corner of the sack through Dextrose cubes for a burst of energy at the end of the day to plastic tubes of honey, pemmican bars, dry fruit, nuts, dry sausage and tea. Obviously some of these are typical lunch items but just make sure you have enough left over to provide emergency rations if for some reason you have to spend an unexpected night out.

The classic lunch and the one most likely on a long trip is the simple combination of some dried meat like salami, liverwurst, smoked ham, tinned or smoked fish, hard bread (such as foil-wrapped pumpernickel), some dried fruit and nuts and a piece of chocolate or other sweet. Water in your canteen may be made more palatable by the addition of powdered fruit mixes. While you may not want to take the time to cook a lunch on a long trip, the mid-day stop on a day tour is often a highlight of the short trip. You will almost certainly have dead wood at hand (or else may carry a small stove) and the burst of heat will be welcome if there is a chill wind blowing.

The leader picks a sheltered spot which will catch the noonday sun and sends members of the party to snap off dry branches while he opens the pack and spreads out a light tarp as a seat. In some cases the fire may be more ceremonial or a source of heat than a necessity for cooking since the cook may have stowed a hearty stew in a thermos and packed it in ready to eat. At the least the thermos will contain a thick soup or may offer a chili, beef stew or any other concoction which will pour into the bottle. This may be backed up with whole wheat bread sandwiches generously loaded with butter and egg, cold meat, cheese or the kids' favorite — peanut butter and jam.

Cookouts can include wieners, hamburgers and those with hearty appetites may want to grill a steak and munch it on a large slice of toast. If the weather is nice you may even want to play around with shishkabobs of meat marinated the night before.

From New Brunswick come three suggestions for meals which can be prepared ahead of time and reheated or cooked over the campfire.

Shirley's beans: a recipe from the Miramichi lumber camps.

The day before the trip start with a crock half full of beans, then add a medium-size onion, one-quarter pound salt pork, three tablespoons of brown sugar, one-half teaspoon of pepper, one teaspoon of salt, one heaping teaspoon of dry mustard, one-half teaspoon of ginger and one-quarter cup plus two tablespoons of molasses. Then fill the crock with more beans. Add boiling water, cover and cook at 350 degrees for seven hours. Since it will be difficult to bring the food hot in the crock you should start a good fire about two hours before lunch time, then place the crock in the embers and heap them around the sides. Then take an hour or so to practice technique or take some photos in the area. At the last minute break out some wieners and roast them over the open fire, then serve the beans with already buttered bread you have wrapped in aluminum and heated at the edge of the fire.

Ragout d'Acadie: an outdoor stew.

The day before the trip prepare the meal. Take one pound each of fat beef ribs and lean stewing beef, cut in pieces, coat with flour, salt and pepper and brown in butter. Place in a pot and add: five medium potatoes cut in quarters, five carrots cut up, one medium turnip cut up, one small onion cut in chunks, one large can of stewed tomatoes, one teaspoon of salt and one teaspoon of pepper. Add water until the pot is half full and boil for one hour. Then add a small cauliflower cut in small pieces and one-half cup of chopped green onions and boil one more hour. This stew also requires an hour or more of cooking in the crock in embers or else a faster heating over a gas stove.

A quicker meal is Carleton County Potato Pancakes.

Prepare ahead of time. Chop up one pound of fresh or frozen fish fillets. Add three beaten eggs, two tablespoons of flour, two tablespoons of grated onion, one tablespoon of chopped parsley, two teaspoons of salt, dashes of nutmeg, pepper and tarragon, two cups of finely grated raw potatoes. Form into patties and wrap in foil. Pack some applesauce. At the campfire fry patties in hot cooking oil for three or four minutes on each side and serve with applesauce.

Liquid refreshment can vary from the Canadian woodsman's classic kettle of tea to the thermos or pot of coffee to the skier's wineskin loaded with whatever suits the individual's taste. However, a change of pace is provided by this recipe, also from New Brunswick:

Keswick Spiced Cider.

For each cup of apple cider add two teaspoons of honey and one-quarter teaspoon each of nutmeg, ginger and lemon juice. Heat until steaming, pour into warmed mugs, then add a cinnamon stick for swizzling. This can also be packed in a thermos for a quick break.

The dessert course can be as simple as a chocolate bar or can range into cakes and cookies provided they are packed in such things as plastic boxes or tins to prevent crumbling. On a day trip you can throw in fresh fruits provided they are wrapped to prevent freezing, a proviso which should be applied to everything. In addition, the wrapping should be done with an eye to prevention of any spills so you will probably use generous amounts of plastic bags. Fuel and stoves should be well wrapped and kept as far away as possible from any foodstuffs.

To these standard menus one can add such specialty items as fresh maple taffy garnered during visits to sugaring off ceremonies at maple bushes during the spring and the fruits of ice fishing which can be devoured on the spot if you have fire and pan or grill.

Breakfast and dinner for the winter camper present a few logistical problems, especially when the cooking is done on a small stove, placed on a piece of ensolite in a tent. A hot cereal dish may be made by mixing powdered milk or diluted tinned cream with water and pouring in an instant cereal. You can enliven this by adding some sugar or dried fruit. Tea can be drunk strongly laced with honey, an advantage for the energy conscious skier. If you have time and fuel there are extensive possibilities in the freeze-dried food range, including scrambled eggs and omelets, with bacon chips and tinned bacon.

The night meal is the major one for wilderness travellers and will also probably be a one pot special because of the fact one dish would be cold before a second could be cooked to make a more traditional dinner. Stews tend to be heavy favorites with a soup base to give the water some extra nourishment, then a starch such as potatoes, noodles or instant rice and possibly some dried vegetables before the meat is added. The meal will probably start with a straight soup, then the stew dish and be rounded off with a chunk of cheese, a handful of nuts and some sweet. Along with the basics consider packing some herbs and spices to add a personal touch. For example, curry powder or tomato sauce will both liven up a stew. And for drinks there are the standard fruit powders plus instant tea or coffee and chocolate. You might experiment with such things as serving jello warm and liquid as a dessert beverage.

Navigation

For the skier accustomed to following well marked and often well-worn trails around a resort, navigation might seem to be a completely unnecessary skill. But the moment he strikes out for a run in bush country, even on a wilderness trail marked by a club, he begins to navigate, whether instinctively or consciously. It may simply mean following a wagon road through a small bush until you hit the concession road and realize it's time to turn back; it may be that you will follow a river bank; or the navigation might simply mean keeping a landmark such as a farmer's windmill in sight.

Such simple methods are adopted almost naturally, even by city dwellers little used to foot travel in the country. The interesting part begins when you make trips of more than a mile or two, and especially when you plunge into heavy bush country where no landmarks are visible. In many cases you will ski into the wild country for a couple of hours, rest and have a bite to eat, then ski back out on your now hardened tracks, enjoying the speed of a packed run.

But what do you do if a wind has kicked up while you were travelling in or if it has started to snow heavily? Your tracks could vanish in less than an hour. Or what do you do if you want to cut the trip short by taking a shortcut to a road you know is only a mile or two away through reasonably open bush country?

Do you trust your "instinct for navigation?" If so, you could be in for a nasty surprise. Most of us like to think we can walk, or ski, a straight line, especially when stone sober; but some scientific tests have proven that people are incapable of holding a true course unless they have some steady clues. When you are wandering between the trees, evading obstacles, or going over rolling countryside, you often see nothing but a constantly changing panorama. In this case you will almost certainly travel in circles, just as lost people do the world over.

Even the apparent natural instinct of a professional guide is nothing more than familiarity with his home ground. It's no different than your ability to navigate through your own living room in pitch dark or your inability to do the same thing in a strange room. You probably recall reading the stories of explorers who regularly picked up native guides in one area, then dismissed them and hired new ones in the next mountain pass.

Seasoned explorers or city dwellers with a little practice, some common sense and cool heads can navigate anywhere with the right equipment. The basic tool is a map. For most cross-country skiers this may simply be a few wiggly lines on a piece of paper representing the routes someone had laid out in a given area. Or it may be a topographic map showing hills and valleys, forest and open land, rivers, roads and other natural features present when the photo mapping plane flew overhead. The topographic sheets, printed by the federal Department of Energy, Mines and Resources and available through many provincial government offices as well, are the most detailed and most useful for wilderness travel. Also useful, particularly in mountain regions, are aerial photos, especially if taken in winter.

Unless you are travelling in country with highly visible landmarks and there is no risk of fog or snow to obliterate them, you need a compass. This is the simplest device available to help you move in a constant direction. Even on familiar terrain a compass can be useful if you want to make a shortcut from one trail to another or cut through the bush to a nearby road. A compass, whether it costs one dollar or over $100, is basically a magnetized piece of metal balanced on a pivot and

Compass selection. From left: precise bearing compass, wrist model, simple pocket compass, lapel pin-on type, rugged compass used in armed forces survival kits.

enclosed in a non-magnetic case of plastic, brass or aluminum. The differences between the dime store and the more expensive varieties include things like sturdier materials, liquid damping, luminosity and sighting devices.

To some degree all these are useful features for the bush traveller, who needs to get an accurate reading in the shortest possible time. A few years ago your compass would have been a simple device, like a pocket watch, with a needle which swung back and forth for several seconds, then shakily settled into one position, which you would accept as North. Then you would look across the compass face for the direction in which you wanted to travel, pick it off the letters and numbers marked around the dial and line up a distant object as best you could.

Modern compasses have liquid-filled capsules which settle the needle into position quickly and many offer sighting devices which allow you to take precise bearings and pinpoint your location on a map. At one time compasses were marked with the cardinal points– north, south, east and west– and the various intercardinal points. These ranged from the simple northeast to north northeast to north by north northeast and so on as navigators tried to give ever more precise directions. Except for the basic directions, this system has been replaced with 360 degree marking. Although you may not automatically react with the word "west" when someone throws the bearing "270 degrees" at you, this is a quicker and more precise method of charting direction. For simplicity's sake, at first just remember north is at 360°, east is 90°, south is 180° and west, 270°.

The traditional compass still has a needle pivoting around the face and one end of the needle is marked with letter N or is colored red, black or blue to indicate north. An increasing number of compasses now have no needle but whole dials which rotate – and they are quicker to read.

The easiest way to keep your compass handy but safe is to hang it around your neck with a light, nylon cord and tuck it under your jacket or sweater. Many wilderness travellers stash a second compass deep inside a pack or pocket as travel insurance. Some designs allow the instrument to be pinned on the front of your jacket or strapped on your wrist like a watch and these are useful if you are following a winding path. With this type be particularly careful to keep the device away from steel or iron objects, such as pocket knives, which can deflect the magnetized needle.

The third tool of navigation is a watch. While skiing there is no easy way to measure how many kilometres you have covered unless someone has marked the trail or you can pinpoint your location on a map. Such travel is usually best measured by the time it takes to cover a given distance, which varies with the individual. A strong, expert skier might slip around a trail in one hour, but a novice could take more than twice as long. After your first trail, you will get an idea of how many kilometres per hour you can cover and from there on, it's a matter of finding how long a given trail is and applying you own rate of travel to estimate how much time you need. With experience you will gain speed and awareness of variables like steepness of terrain, snow conditions and the need for rest stops. In a group never forget that the speed and range of your trip are governed by the slowest, weakest member of the party. On a day trip, set a point of no return on your watch and obey it as a pilot would his fuel gauge. If you start at 1 P.M. and darkness falls at 5 P.M., you should be at least half way around a loop by 3 P.M. or turn back at that time.

In a pinch, a watch (though not a digital model) can serve as a crude compass. If you aim the hour hand in the direction of the sun, South will lie directly between the hour hand and 12 on the dial. For example, if it is 8 A.M., South will lie directly over the numberal ten on the watch. At noon, the sun will be sitting directly over the direction South.

If you are going to be bashing around in the bush and possibly falling in the snow, you should have a shockproof and waterproof timepiece on your wrist. Although you may not be tempted to wear a dress watch into the woods or to buy an armored skindiver's model for a few trips only, you might consider a cheap but rugged pocket watch which can be secured to a belt loop or safety pin with a length of nylon cord.

Beyond this basic equipment you should include a map case. It can be as simple as a clear plastic bag or could be one of the plastic envelopes with self-sealing openings, neck cords and pencil pockets sold in many outdoors shops for three to four dollars. Inside this you may toss a six-inch, clear, plastic ruler or blow another four dollars on one of those handy devices which you can roll across the map, especially around curves, to get a quicker measurement. For more precise navigation you might even include a small protractor, which can be placed on the map to provide compass bearings.

Along with the basic equipment you should pick up and commit to memory a few basic skills, increasing the number as your trips become more challenging. Trail marking is probably as old as human settlement and no doubt the cave dwellers scuffed some marks in the dirt with their toes or broke off a few branches as they walked along to mark a return route to shelter or food. Primitive trail markers, such as axe blazes on trees, are still popular in folklore but are losing favor with people like foresters, who see them as open sores, inviting infection of the trees. Other natural systems include stone or snow cairns on open ground, marks scratched on rock faces and pointers made from wood and attached to a pole stuck in the ground.

Now more permanent, more visible and less damaging markers such as paint blazes, fluorescent painted metal or plastic strips or signs and lengths of orange surveyor's tape mark well-used trails. At a resort it is usually enough to follow these markers, remembering to keep following the right color after every intersection in the trails. If you are laying a trail, don't forget to mark both sides of every tree or you will have a one-way route and a devil of a time finding your way back. On more complicated routes you may also need a map to help you pick your way through interconnecting trail networks and again it is often just a case of matching the color of the line on a map to the color of the markers.

Once you start heading for little used trails or try some bushwhacking on your own to explore the back country it is time to learn some details about maps and how to use them. In a pinch you can make your own maps and they may be all you need. At the very least, you will probably have a general road map of any given area of the country and from this can create your own local map with a pencil and piece of paper. It's not a bad idea to carry a pencil and notepad when visiting a resort for the first time, since some owners only post a map at the entrance and if you want a copy you'll have to sketch it there.

A highway map will give you a general outline of the settlements, roads, and large watercourses in an area, but it will not provide the details useful for locating yourself over distances of a few miles. Sometimes you can sketch a simple map, but many times you don't have all the details. For this you need the topographic maps. At first glance, these sheets of lines, names and numbers can be intimidating. In addition to the usual lines for roads and railways, they are covered with a grid of blue lines and a mass of wavy brown lines which seem to wander all over the place.

The blue vertical and horizontal lines, each ending in a number, are used by professionals such as surveyors and pilots to plot exact locations and communicate them in a simple, numerical form. For most travellers, the fact that the lines form a grid makes it easy to calculate rough distances, especially if they are on north-south or east-west routes.

The wavy, brown lines are called contour lines. These are the map-maker's way of translating the hills and dales of the countryside into something readable on a flat surface. Spaces between the lines indicate a change in elevation, such as twenty-five feet on detailed maps. With some practice, you will learn to translate a closely set series of lines into a steep hillside and a series of rough circles into a hilltop. For skiers planning trips across unfamiliar country, such maps are invaluable because they show the steepness of the terrain and suggest routes around cliffs and up gently terraced valleys. With a pencil and compass, you can plot a route across a map on the living room table and be prepared for the twists and turns of the trip even before you snap on your skis.

If you are unfamiliar with the topo sheets as they are sometimes called, it's a good idea to get one of the area where you live or holiday and to try navigating with it as you travel along familiar roads. This will give you the feel for translating directions and spotting such features as hills and buildings from the symbols on a map.

In the Canadian topographic series there are two scales of map which will be of greatest use. The 1:125,000 scale (one inch on the map equals 125,000 inches on the ground or about two miles) is handy for locating general areas such as river and lake systems and simply for getting the lay of the land. The 1:50,000 series (1 ¼ inches to 1 mile) is the type most commonly used for actual wilderness travel, since it locates just about every creek and cabin in the bush.

Topo maps and free indexes and map lists are available from the Canada Map Office, 615 Booth St., Ottawa, Ontario, K1A 0E9. Maps also can be obtained through provincial government departments responsible for recreation, conservation and natural resources and from map dealers across the country. The Canada Map Office can provide you with a complete list of suppliers.

Once you have the tools for the job, you need to learn some fundamental skills of navigation. Basic but commonly overlooked is a method of finding your way

Wilderness travel demands the ability to navigate, usually by map and compass.

back to a starting point if there is no obvious landmark. It may sound silly, but you can travel all day into the bush, then back to the road where you started and find yourself "lost." This will happen when you work your way back to the road satisfactorily (by reversing the compass bearing you took on the inbound leg of the trip) but have enough deviation in your return course to be out of sight of your car. In such a case you won't know whether to turn left or right to walk down the road to the vehicle. The problem becomes even more difficult when the point you are returning to is a single target such as a cabin.

In each case, you either have to find or create a base line. You may have a natural base line such as a road, railway, lake, river, hydro line or cliff which is close enough to your return point that it will serve as a signpost when you head back. If no such line exists you may have to create one. In the bush you can string a long series of blazes– with colored tape around trees– out for a mile or more in two or even four directions from a base camp. Just make sure they indicate which way leads back to camp. In open country you might have to firmly plant tall, colorfully marked stakes. Whatever system you use just make sure the markers are close enough together that you won't wander through the base line without spotting the indicators.

From that base line you will take a line of travel at right angles to head into the bush or the mountains. For example, the base line might be a river which runs east and west and you will head due north from a cabin on the river bank for a day of exploring the bush. Coming back may be as simple as following your ski tracks in the snow or it may be complicated by newly fallen snow or you may simply want to try another route back. In this case, you should not try to simply reverse the direction and head due south because the twists and turns you will make in rough country could put you off course enough to end up on either side of the cabin. It's safer to make an intentional deviation of several degrees so that when you hit the base line you know which way to turn to head for the cabin and a hot supper.

If you have a sighting method on your compass and some prominent landmarks, you will be able to navigate with more confidence by creating lines of position or by using triangulation to locate yourself. A line of position is like one of the latitude or longitude lines already drawn on a map. You can create your own lines of position using a compass and landmarks. At your starting point or base camp take a precise compass bearing on some prominent object, such as a distinctive hilltop or mountain peak which lies in your general direction of travel for the day. You might, for example, get a reading of 50 degrees. Then you could strike out on a wandering course and whenever you wanted to get a precise route back to the starting point simply keep moving until you reached a place where you could get a bearing of 50 degrees on the mountain. As long as you moved in such a way that you kept that bearing you would be on a line between camp and the mountain.

In another case you might be lost but have a map of an area and be able to see some distinctive natural features. Here it would help to have a compass with a sight and a straight edge for marking lines or else a ruler and protractor. You would take a bearing on one target, such as the lone mountain peak in an area, and would trace a line on the map from that peak at the same angle as your compass reading. To place yourself more precisely you would need a second and if possible, a third bearing, perhaps on a distant waterfall and a lake you would also locate on the map. Where the lines intersected on the map is where you would be. This is triangulation.

Before striking out to navigate with a new compass, you should have a basic understanding of how it really operates. The needle of a magnetic compass rarely points to true north. Actually, the needle aligns itself with the Earth's magnetic field at the point where it is being used and even this field doesn't run in straight lines like the grid on a map. Instead, it fans out in curving lines from a fifty square mile area on Bathurst Island in northern Canada. Only along the agonic line, which runs from magnetic North south through Lake Superior, is the magnetic pole more or less in line with true north.

In Newfoundland and British Columbia, the variation (or declination, as it is technically known) is thirty degrees and in parts of the far north, it is so great that a magnetic compass is difficult or even impossible to use with any accuracy. So unless you live in Ontario or Manitoba, the declination from true north is going to vary enough that you should consider it when navigating from maps. In the case of topographic sheets you will find the declination marked and graphically illustrated in a corner of the map and you can make appropriate corrections to your compass readings. If you are east of the agonic line, you will add the number of degrees of declination for your area to any bearing you get to have a true bearing for use on a map. If you are in the west, you will subtract for a correction.

If you live on the east or west coast, you might consider getting a compass with a small screw to make semi-permanent corrections for declination. This will save you the time of adding or subtracting a certain number of degrees from each bearing. In serious navigation, declination should not be overlooked because a difference of twenty degrees could put you in the wrong pass of a mountain range.

Two skiers pause for a moment to watch a fresh snowfall at the edge of a sheltering woodland.

However, if you are simply heading into the bush for a day, without a detailed map of the area, it is usually sufficient to take a simple bearing from your base line and follow that in.

Navigation by natural signs is a favorite topic of camp counsellors, who can explain in great detail how you can take bearings from Polaris, the North Star, or from the sun or from moss on trees. Of these the North Star is the most faithful compass but is not particularly handy since you have to wait till dark and a clear night at that. If you are still out and lost at dark, you will probably be huddled in some temporary shelter trying to keep warm.

The sun does lie due south at noon, but it does not regularly rise in the east or set in the west. In winter it travels from a point somewhere in the southeast to a point somewhere in the southwest quadrant of the sky, while in summer it will be north of east and west. So navigation by the sun can lack precision, but it will give you a general idea of the directions and that may even be enough to get you back to something like a familiar trail. Even when the sun is obscured by clouds there are ways of finding it. On skis you can sometimes do this by skiing across a clearing. The side of the clearing where your skis sink the deepest will be the north side because this will have received the most heat from the sun. The south side would be crustier because it was shaded by trees.

There are other natural features and signs which you will pick up, particularly when you become familiar with an area or on how to pick up details from topo sheets. For example, you might come to a river you know flows from east to west. If the water is open or you can bash a hole in the ice, you will get a peek at the current.

Most Canadians are familiar with methods of finding their ways around built-up areas. Navigation off the beaten path isn't that much more difficult, it's just different and it takes some practice. You can pick up some good experience just using a map and compass in familiar areas to get the feel of these tools and, if the idea appeals to you, consider joining one of the orienteering clubs which make navigation on foot or on skis a weekend sport.

Two useful reference books which deal with navigation in detail are: *The Wilderness Route Finder,* by Calvin Rutstrum and *Be Expert with Map and Compass,* by Bjorn Kjellstrom.

Winter Survival

A ski trail leading to a remote campsite.

In recent years the word survival has taken on new meanings as legions of city dwellers head for the wilderness and find they lack the skills common to the most primitive aborigines. This discovery has spawned a whole new industry, the survival school, as people used to ready-made food, clothing, shelter and heat struggle to re-learn abilities lost over generations of urban life. The concept of survival as a skill which can be taught over a short period of time seems to have its roots in the military training exercises which began in the Second World War. For example, the Outward Bound schools trace their roots to training sessions given sailors to help them survive at sea if their ships were torpedoed.

Various types of survival courses were and still are given to airmen who might have to ditch in uninhabited areas and to troops trained to penetrate and live far behind enemy lines. In postwar years a few military veterans gave similar courses privately, usually to hunters and fishermen. During the 1960s, as wilderness sports like hiking, canoeing, snowmobiling and cross-country skiing became popular, the number of these courses increased sharply and the whole concept of survival training gained considerable publicity. Now it is common to see articles on survival in newspapers and magazines, programs on television and survival courses offered in such institutions as community colleges.

Often "survival" is an overdramatic word for what is being taught. Actually the students are usually learning the basics of wilderness living: the sort of techniques often used by our own ancestors as little as a century ago and still part of the life of many northern dwellers. A businessman used to nothing more rigorous than commuting through the occasional snowstorm and shovelling his driveway would be risking his life to go for a walk in the Arctic, even if he packed all the right equipment. An Eskimo walking just over the next ice ridge however, might use a piece of bone shaped like a crude saw to cut snow blocks for an igloo, light a koodlik lamp fueled with fat, munch some seal meat or fish and sleep comfortably, wrapped in animal skins.

As more and more people born and bred in cities follow the urge to rediscover nature and particularly to explore its frozen beauty on skis, they need to learn some of the ways of wilderness life. At the least these may keep them warm and dry some stormy night when they can't make it back to permanent shelter. These skills might even save them from frostbite or worse.

The most important thing you can take into the wilderness is a cool head and a realistic but positive attitude toward your own abilities. This survival psychology means recognizing your own limitations and not tackling a route beyond your own capabilities, but at the same time, not losing hope if you become lost or injured. Armed forces instructors say people cope better with survival situations if they are prepared for the idea. Reading about techniques, and particularly practicing them, help people to form some mental attitudes and absorb some skills which will be ready if they are ever needed. On the other hand, your worst enemies include irrational fear and hopelessness, which can let you give up fighting even though your body could carry on.

Sometimes you can draw hope by remembering tales of endurance and survival by explorers and marooned travellers who used whatever tools they could make or find to build shelters, find food and even improvise means of travel.

If you are in a group, and you should be if you are touring in the back country, you should either have or adopt a sense of group psychology if the going gets tough. There may be a natural leader, often the most experienced outdoorsman in the group, and he should give direction to the less experienced members. He may direct one person to gather material for shelter building, another to find dry wood for a fire and someone else to organize the equipment so nothing will be lost or soaked in the wet snow.

The possibility of facing some kind of survival situation should not be ignored by anyone. Conceivably you could become at least temporarily lost in a storm and have to bivouac overnight without a tent and sleeping bag or someone in the group might shatter a ski or suffer an injury, delaying the return.

First you should study and, if possible, practice some of the basic wilderness skills such as finding or making shelter and fire. These two things will enable you to last several days even with no food and little water. This doesn't necessarily mean enrolling in a course. There are many good books on the subject and plenty of open country in which to try your hand with these new skills.

Another key to surviving in case of accident can be getting help in a hurry. Help can only come if someone is missing you and knows where to send a rescue party. Many long and costly search and rescue missions could have been eliminated if people heading into the wilds had taken a minute to leave word with a friend, relative or even at an official post such as a ranger station. You should leave specific details of the route you plan to take and when you expect to return, making some sort of allowance for minor delays.

Equipment

Before leaving on any trip you should prepare some equipment as outlined in the chapter on touring and winter camping. Of course you need a map of the area and a compass and the knowledge of how to use them. A sharp, well-sheathed hatchet should be stashed somewhere in your rucksack. With this primitive but highly efficient tool you can cut small trees to make a lean-to shelter and chop up dead branches for fuel. For many outdoorsmen of a traditional bent, the axe is the last tool they would give up. Of course if you are beyond the tree line, in the mountains or far north, you will replace the hatchet with a snow saw for cutting blocks of snow. With these you can make a snow shelter or even an igloo.

In addition to the hatchet you can pack a knife, which will serve for making tinder from dry wood, repairing damaged wood skis and slicing your dry sausage. A useful type is the Swiss Army knife, loaded with such tools as screwdrivers, awls and even hacksaws. Matches of course are essential and you should carry them in at least two, separate, waterproof packages. The first package will be for lighting campfires or your stove at lunch as you would normally expect to. The second is an emergency reserve. Use ordinary "strike anywhere" matches and avoid the "windproof" and "waterproof" types that need special surfaces for ignition. If the surface is damaged the matches are useless.

If you feel at all unsure about your capabilities at fire and shelter making, you could pack a pocketbook on survival in a plastic bag. If all else fails the paper will make good tinder. A better idea for tinder is to stash a few of the dry, solid barbecue fire starter cubes in a couple of layers of plastic or to use a candle stub.

A first aid kit can mean the difference between returning from the trip with a minor discomfort or being immobilized. For starters you should read a good book on wilderness first aid or at least the St. John Ambulance manual. Then adopt a packing list in such a book or adapt it to your own needs. As a minimum you will need bandages, scissors, tweezers, disinfectant, ointment and painkillers.

A repair kit will contain such items as brass wire and strong tape for making emergency repairs to equipment, several binding screws, screwdriver and pocket tool for making holes in the skis to allow repairs. Of course you should carry a spare ski tip and might look for the metal type which incorporates a folding snow saw. In addition to your normal lunch you will add at least a small emergency ration for everyone. This might include an extra length of sausage, chocolate bars and some Dextrose tablets.

If you are well equipped, a night on the trail will be more of an adventure than a true survival experience.

Time
Time is the biggest factor in creating many of these unexpected nights out. Some skiers simply overestimate the ability of themselves or others in the group to complete a long circuit in wild country. They fail to make allowances for heavy snow and muscles not used to the strain of such a trip. Some time in the late afternoon the leader should take a hard look at the time, should know when darkness will fall and must estimate whether it is safe or even possible to make a dash for home. If not, the party is better to take the last few minutes of light in searching out a good location for a camp and making preparations for a night out.

Shelter
Shelter is the first priority. If you know what to look for and what to do, there should be little problem. For example, just remember the last time you were walking in the woods when a shower struck and you found dry shelter beneath a thick pine or spruce. The heavy boughs of a coniferous tree will give you shelter from wind and snow during a winter's night.

At the very least you might dig under the snow-laden limbs of the largest, thick-

The classic woodland survival shelter, a lean-to made of branches with a mattress of spruce boughs and a reflector fire in front.

est tree you can spot and find a place with only a thin layer of snow. Or you might discover a huge tree recently blown down and still holding its needles. You can trim off a few branches to make an opening (away from the prevailing wind of course) and snuggle under. Assuming you haven't forgotten a good supply of matches, the best shelter will be a classic lean-to facing a fire.

If it is to shelter only yourself, look for a couple of trees about seven feet apart and with level ground between them so you can stretch out under the roof you are about to build. Cut a ridgepole, and wedge that between the branches of the two trees about four feet from the ground. If no supporting trees are available, you can brace one or both ends of the shelter with a bipod or tripod arrangement of sticks lashed together at their tops.

When the ridgepole is secure, lean the roof support poles about one foot apart and at a forty-five degree angle to the ridgepole. Then thatch the roof with a six to twelve-inch layer of coniferous branches which you can easily strip off with your hands. Start at the bottom of the shelter and with the tips of the branches facing the ground, work your way up to the top with each layer of branches overlapping the layer below. Then thatch in both sides of the shelter.

Next you will build a floor or "browse bed" of soft evergreen branches, both to give you a decent mattress for the night and to insulate you from the cold below. Lay at least a six-inch layer with the bottom sides of the branches up so the sharp butt ends will be face down. If you have the time, lay a log in front of the bed both to keep the branches in place and to give you a place to sit.

While you collect wood for the shelter, you should also lay in a supply of dead wood for a fire. If you have enough fuel, you should build a fire the length of the shelter to warm your entire body.

This is the style for a one-man shelter. If more than one person is going to spend the night there, it will have to be deep enough so each person can sleep with either their head or feet toward the fire.

Of course if you have packed a light, nylon tarpaulin it will be much easier to rig an emergency shelter and it will be more windproof. If you thought to add a reflective-coated blanket, this will make the floor more secure and draft-proof and will help bounce back your body's heat. A few people, usually those with mountaineering experience, carry a bivouac bag, which is a large sack into which you can stuff yourself and sleeping bag, if you have it, to pass a night out of the wind.

Another type of natural shelter sometimes available is the cave. This is solid protection but not always easy to find and often damp or lined with sharp rocks or boulders. At times it is already inhabited. However, it you are travelling in hilly country where the snow is deep, you can make your own cave in the snow and pass a night undisturbed by the wildest blizzard. The only problem is that it takes several hours and some effort to build a good shelter. But if you are stuck for the night and have your flashlight handy, you can dig at least a respectable one.

A snow cave is shaped like a classic igloo but is carved, instead of built out of snow. Ideally, you should tunnel into a thick bank of snow, then start scooping out a dome-shaped room. This is a wet job and you should wear a parka and overpants. It is also slow going with hands alone and easier done with a small shovel. Once inside, poke one or two small ventilation holes through the roof and protect the entrance from drifting in with some snow blocks to act as a snow fence.

The cave will be warmest if you keep the tunnel entrance low and carve out a sleeping platform a foot or two higher up. Snow is a good insulator of course, as the relative warmth of the cave will show. But it is cold to sit on directly. If you have no branches or insulating pads to put beneath your body, use a packsack or even plastic bags to ease the chill. Don't worry about freezing to death in your sleep; the cold will wake you up first and you'll toss, turn and if lightly clad, shiver a bit to turn a few more calories of fat into body heat.

On flat snow, such as on a glacier or in the Arctic, you may have to make a trench or igloo. The trench is simply a ditch dug a couple of feet or more deep and covered with whatever is handy. If there is at least some brush handy, you might use some of it to line the bottom of the shelter and the rest to make a roof with the aid of skis and poles. On top of that you would add a layer of snow to make it windproof. Or if there is no shrubbery at all you could carve snow blocks from the packed surface and lean them against one another to form a peaked roof. If the snow is too shallow even for that, you may have to cut snow block walls and roof them with other snow slabs.

Igloo building takes even more time than cave-digging and it's the sort of thing you might want to practice. The secret is to create an ever ascending spiral of snow blocks rather than simply laying rows as you would brick up a house. Obviously you have to bevel the blocks and gently tap them into place so they will hold. A snow saw and knife are a necessity and a detailed description of the technique is helpful. There are good instructions in the Canadian Forces booklet *Down but Not Out,* a paperback on survival for stranded airmen.

Keeping Warm

Keeping warm while you are holed up for the night is important. Certainly you want to prevent any of your extremities from suffering frostbite and, if possible, you also want to get some sleep (for which you'll need to prevent an excessive loss of body heat).

In cross-country skiing you generate a steady flow of heat so that you need little clothing while on the move. A few moments after you stop moving, the last of that excess heat will have evaporated and been blown away by the wind. You will probably react by pulling your toque down over your ears and the back of your neck and putting up the hood of your jacket if there is one. Then you will switch to warm mitts and pull on overpants to insulate your legs. The down or polyester filled ski jacket will go on over your light jacket.

As the cold moves in, your feet will probably feel it first. Unless you had room for a pair of mukluks in the day pack, you won't have much extra insulation. Look around and use your imagination. Once you have settled in place for a while, you could partially fill the packsack with the tips of pine branches, slip your feet inside and draw the top snug around your calves. Then pull the nylon tarp or space blanket around your body to act as a further windbreak and toss another couple of sticks on the fire.

Remember, it's the thickness that insulates you against the loss of body heat and in a pinch, you can even stuff pine needles, bark, moss, feathers, animal skins or just about anything else you can lay your hands on under your jacket or around your shelter. The great enemies of any insulator are wind and water. Wind, as you can tell by its effects on your face, wipes away the heat as fast as it can radiate. One answer is to wear a windproof outer shell, such as nylon or one of the cotton-nylon weaves, and the second is to get out of the wind as fast as you can.

Water can hit you from both sides. On the average the body evaporates 1 ½ pints of water– almost one litre– per day. That moisture can clog the tiny air cells in any clothing, especially down-filled, and act as a heat conductor. To avoid that, you need clothing which is water resistant (but not waterproof, most of the time) to allow evaporation right through to the outside and you need to be able to zip open your clothing when heat builds up. On the other hand, you may need highly water resistant or even waterproof clothing such as a poncho or cagoule if you could hit rain.

You just may not be able to keep your feet completely dry during the day and the best answer is to have at least one pair of dry socks stuffed away in the pack.

Fire

The answer to your heat problems of course is fire. On a long trip you will have a gas stove and several aluminum Sigg bottles topped up with fuel, but on a day trip you might carry nothing more than a couple of waterproof containers of matches. Such brass and nickel containers are available in many sporting goods stores or you might use one of these as an absolutely safe package and use a more capacious thirty-five mm film container for the main holder.

Primitive methods of fire building look good in books and may be fun to practice during the summer when you have an afternoon to while away, but they should not be counted on under adverse conditions when you need heat in a hurry and everything around you is wet. Here it helps even to carry some fire starter such as barbecue cubes or a candle or even a couple of pieces of Kleenex. Then you need a large pile of dry wood such as the dead, lower branches which can be snapped off most trees and the frequent dead tree you will find in real forest.

As you gather your wood you try to get at least three thicknesses. The tiniest, driest twigs you can find in sheltered places around tree trunks will be your most likely fire starter. If necessary, you can make fuzz sticks by starting but not cutting free a series of shavings on a stick from which you have removed the damp bark. Of course, the woodsman's emergency fuel source in many places is the birch tree, one of the few woods which will burn even when it is wet. You wouldn't strip a tree unless it was an emergency any more than you would slash pines to make a lean-to, unless your safety depended on it– but these are the things you should know about just in case you need them. The fine birch bark will make an excellent tinder and the branches will burn fiercely.

The next size of fuel will be pencil-thick branches or heavier branches split open with a knife or hatchet to expose their dry interiors. Then come the heavy

Mike Exall, ski and survival instructor at Toronto's Seneca College, coaxes life from a fire with a few full breaths of air.

pieces, including small logs and even stumps to hold the heat through the night. You will have stamped down the snow in the area of your camp, but the heat of a fire will melt the snow and your sticks will disappear if they don't have some sort of base.

The most secure base would be a platform of rocks, but you'll probably have to settle for a double or triple layer of green branches which will be slow to burn through. If you can build your shelter about four or five feet from a cliff or even a snowbank, you will have a natural reflector. Otherwise you can improvise a reflector by stacking birch branches or peeled sticks between upright stakes on the far side of your blaze. With a full-length fire in front of a well-made lean-to, you can spend a reasonably comfortable night. As the fire dies down from time to time, the chill will awaken you long enough to throw a few more logs on the embers and you'll roll over to warm your other side. You should automatically store some dry tinder in a secure corner of your sleeping quarters in case you have to re-light the fire in the morning and you should cover your dry firewood with a few evergreen branches to keep it clear of snow which could fall during the night.

When you awaken in the morning you will appreciate a hot drink and to make one you'll need a metal container. Some outdoorsmen pack some of their supplies in a coffee or nut can which has a plastic top and with a piece of wire they can rig a handle, then suspend it over the fire with a stick. At the least you will need a metal cup to melt some snow and boil up some tea from the bag you slipped into your emergency food packet.

Accidents and first aid

Cross-country skiing is not considered a high-risk sport, but if you take to bushwhacking there is a chance that some day you will run into something solid, get caught in a severe cold snap or will damage your equipment. Equipment breakage can range from the annoying to the serious. For example, shattering a bamboo ski pole will be unsettling at the least and could cause an injury if you fall on the splintered shaft. But you may be able to repair the damaged pole in a few minutes with the strong tape you carry. Otherwise you might settle for a slightly slower pace and just keep going with one pole. If you still have a long distance to cover, you can simply cut yourself another pole from a handy sapling, taking time to slide the basket from the old pole onto the new one.

A damaged ski is more serious. Tip breakage is the most common problem if a wood ski rams a rock or tree trunk and this is often quickly repaired by sliding on an emergency ski tip. If for some reason you forgot to pack one, you may have to resort to the trick of sliding a mitt over the end of the ski or to some fancy taping and bracing with jury-rigged splints.

Should a ski be shattered by a severe fall, you may have to start using some imagination and whatever gear you packed in your repair kit. For example, you may be able to lash the tail back in place with tape or spare screws and a rough board cut from a small tree. Theoretically, you could even hack a new ski from some dead hardwood, steaming the tip over a boiling billy of water to bend it up; but this would be time consuming and possibly dangerous unless you had adequate food and shelter. Some bush dwellers have rigged their own snowshoes in an emergency, using bent saplings and whatever lacing material they could find or create. Again this is not a task to be started lightly, for you will have to make the webbing strong enough to take your weight.

Personal injury is something you don't want to dwell on but should be prepared for. Many problems can be avoided by a few simple precautions. For example, if you are skiing in heavy brush and especially if you are tackling some downhill sections, slide your hands out of your pole straps. This could save you from a nasty dislocation if a pole basket should snag something. Frostbite, particularly on an exposed face, is a possibility when you are skiing on cold days, particularly if there is a sharp wind whistling out of the north. In such weather, a hood tied under the chin, a scarf across the face or possibly a balaclava wool face mask will save you problems. For extreme climates there are even down-filled masks.

The simplest ways to avoid frostbite are to stop and warm your face if you feel it getting very cold and for members of a group to watch each other's faces for the telltale white blotches indicating frostbite. Unless you are in a state of collapse or woefully underdressed for the climate, there is little excuse for getting a serious case of frostbite on your extremities. If you are starting to lose sensation in your hands, simply put on the warm mitts you carry in your day pack. Or at the least jam them under your armpits where they will find plenty of warmth. In the case of feet, try skiing faster or simply bouncing up and down on your skiis or even taking off your skis and doing a quick dance on the hard snow. The problem might also be wet socks and it might be time to change to the dry pair in your pack. If someone in your party has feet that are turning white with frostbite, get the warmest member of the group to take those feet under his armpits or against his stomach until they thaw out.

By now everyone should know that rubbing snow on frostbite will do more harm than good. If you have a case of serious frostbite on your hands and the flesh is frozen solid, avoid rubbing anything on the skin since this will only damage the hardened tissue. The skier should be evacuated – walking or skiing if necessary, on a frozen foot – to a place where the frozen part can be kept in water of about forty-two degrees Celsius or 108 Farenheit until thawed and where there is no danger of re-freezing. Treat a frostbitten part as you would a burn by wrapping it in a sterile dressing. The patient should be given extra clothing, warm drinks and food.

Hypothermia is the new catchword among outdoorsmen and is a more accurate term to describe what we once called exposure. It is Greek for "too little heat" and expresses what happens to the body when it is losing heat faster than it can be regenerated by burning food and fat reserves. It is more serious than frostbite since it involves a chilling of the body's core and can be a killer even in above freezing temperatures. Most people have had a brush with it when they got caught in a cold, driving rainstorm with only light clothing and suddenly found themselves shivering uncontrollably. If the heat loss continues past a certain point, the heart begins to beat aimlessly and death follows.

Violent and uncontrollable shivering is a good sign of hypothermia. So are poor co-ordination, which often shows up in a slow and stumbling pace, thick, slurred speech and a deep feeling of cold and numbness – all of which can impair the ability to react wisely to the impending problem.

All outdoors travellers should react to these signs and if one member of a party is starting to show them, get that person warmed up fast. Usually the two major problems are dampness wicking away heat from the body and wind evaporating it from there on. If there are fresh dry clothes, put them on and get out of the wind. Hot food and drink are the best cures, but shared body heat, nude body to nude body in a sleeping bag also makes a quick heat transfer and will help bring someone around. Like frostbite, hypothermia is the sort of thing that should not happen to a properly equipped and led party, but might easily be an additional problem for someone stranded or already suffering shock from an injury.

Anyone who travels on ice during the winter is taking a risk of dunking. At the worst this may only mean a wet foot as you scamper and slide to safety, but even this can pose serious problems. One immediate solution is to immediately roll the wet part of your body in dry, powder snow if available, as this will blot up some of the water. With luck and reasonably water-repellent clothing, you may end up with nothing worse than an armour plating of ice which can be brushed and scraped away. However, you will more likely have to find some immediate shelter, get into any dry clothing available and possibly build a fire.

Snow blindness should not be a problem for any skier equipped with a good pair of sunglasses, preferably of dark glass if you travel in the high country. If you do find your eyes swollen and sore after a day on the snow, you should have some antiseptic eye ointment in your medicine kit to ease the problem. Somehow your sunglasses may be lost or broken and you don't have another pair in your pack. In this case you may have to make your own eye protectors by tying a strip of some material such as nylon or even tree bark in front of your eyes and cutting small slits for vision. Of course you will have to travel carefully because of your limited vision.

Sunburn can be a serious problem in spring skiing or at high altitudes, where there is less filtration of the sun's rays. Every skier should carry one of the tiny tubes of suntan lotion available in drugstores and ski shops and should get a sunscreen lotion if touring at high altitudes in the spring.

Another problem for high altitude parties is mountain sickness or the more serious high-altitude, pulmonary edema. Altitude sickness can strike most people not used to the change in elevation, but again most people become acclimatized to it. Edema is usually only a problem in high ranges (above 10,000 feet) and involves fluid building up in the lungs. Immediate evacuation to a lower altitude is the cure.

Other injuries which might strike a skier are dislocations and fractures. Often it is better to try to replace a dislocated bone in a socket and endure a few seconds of extra pain rather than try to hobble back on the trail. In the case of fractures, someone will have to splint the injury as best possible with bandages or possibly with a splint made from a split open tree branch. A broken arm may be lashed to the torso and one broken leg to the other good one in a pinch. If you carry in your pack a piece of wire mesh splint made for such emergency use, then things may be a lot easier.

Under such circumstances you may have to organize an evacuation of the injured person. Unless you are so well equipped that you have a roll-up sled, you will have to help the victim walk or ski out or you must rig some kind of sleigh. It won't be easy, but with tape and nylon cord, the skis and ski poles of the injured party and some branches, you can fashion a crude sled. This should be padded with extra clothing, sleeping bags and even branches to make it more comfortable. The rider should be well dressed and wrapped in a waterproof tarpaulin if possible.

There are many publications on survival and if you are interested in the outdoors, you will probably want to obtain at least a couple for reference. Among useful works are: *Down but Not Out,* the Canadian Armed Forces manual already mentioned; several of the Bradford Angier series of books, including *How to Stay Alive in the Woods, Skills for Taming the Wilds* and *Being Your Own Wilderness Doctor; Wilderness Skiing* by Lito Tejada-Flores and Allen Steck, published by the Sierra Club; *First Aid,* the manual of the St. John Ambulance Association.

The following is a suggested list for a toilet and first aid kit. You may want to add some personal medications such as those for allergies. Never count on being able to buy what you need on the road. The kits should be packed in metal or tightly closing plastic boxes.

Toilet Kit
suntan lotion
Uval (total sunscreen)
Solarcaine (sunburn lotion)
sewing kit of needles, threads and thimble
cuticle scissors
nail clippers
nail file
tweezers
comb
metal mirror with cord for hanging and hole in middle for emergency signalling plus instructions for signalling.
toothbrush
toothpaste tube, in plastic bag
safety pins
toilet paper
Kleenex
plastic tube of liquid soap

First Aid Kit
disinfectant (such as Merthiolate)
cream for cuts and scrapes (such as Ozonol)
222s or 292s if you can get a prescription
ASA tablets for a mild headache
tetracycline (or other antibiotic)
opthalmic ointment
sleeping tablets
Lomotil
triangular bandages
tensor bandage
2 inch bandages
bandaids
gauze compresses
2 inch roll of tape
eye pads
sterile plastic bags
St. John Ambulance First Aid manual

The Elements of Winter

"Mon pays c'est l'hiver," (my country it is the winter) sings Quebec songwriter Gilles Vigneault.

Canada has been given – some would say blessed and some would say cursed – with one of the snowiest climates of any country in the world. On Rocky Mountain glaciers and in the high Arctic you can find snow, some of it skiable, all year round. Excepting such balmy spots as the southwestern corners of Ontario and British Columbia, the land is white for upwards of three months each year.

Anywhere from September to October snow makes its first, somewhat hesitant appearance. One cool autumn day a few snowflakes drift down from a slate-colored sky – vanguards of the billions to come in the months ahead. From then until the hot sun of May hunts down and melts the final patches huddled on north slopes and deep in the bush we will walk in it, shovel it, try not to get stuck in it and hopefully find some idyllic minutes playing in it.

For the skier even winter has its seasons. At first there is a tempting little layer of snow on the ground when you awake one morning in late fall. It is time to step up the tempo of that exercise program you have been toying with since late September when the canoe and packsacks were stored. You gauge the snow still a bit too thin even for a run across a nearby golf course and settle for a check of equipment. Are the skis tarred, the boots waxed and the long johns where you can find them? How is the wax kit? Maybe it's time to replace that stub of violet you nursed through last spring. You settle down one evening with a pile of maps and start planning some tours for this winter, then you reach for the phone book wondering who might be interested in joining a trip.

That first layer will melt away but soon be replaced by more determined snowfalls. In the short days of early winter you head out, watching for rocks and stubs of pruned underbrush just beneath this thin snow cover. The fields are full of weeds, their heads still laden with seeds not yet buried by the snow. You skirt the thin ice of streams and rivers but look for broken areas which indicate a beaver or muskrat has been passing by.

January and the cold reaches its deepest point. Some days it is so cold you don't venture farther than a nearby park where you join dozens of newcomers to the sport testing their Christmas present ski outfits and making tentative attempts at kick and glide. Other days you try tours in forests, counting on the trees to break the force of the bitter north wind. Even so, you carry a down-filled parka and warm-up pants for the lunch break in a thick pine grove. With little encouragement a gray Canada Jay flutters in to take a handful of bread crumbs. Then you finish the thermos of tea and head back for the road, listening as you go to the trees creak in the wind and the cold, dry snow echoing the sound from beneath your feet.

By February and March your leg muscles will be firmed up and your wind capable of sustained runs through the heavy snows which now blanket everything in sight. The days are a bit longer and warmer and you poke through the bush, following the characteristic two wide, two narrow tracks of a rabbit you flushed from its hiding place under a spruce. You deliberately detour through a grove of apple trees, hoping to flush a grouse and as usual, the bird spots you first and the sudden burst of sound from its frantic wing-beats jumps your heartbeat. With temperatures a bit milder, you join the ever increasing numbers taking a week or two of winter vacation and looking for a friendly lodge with trails for good excur-

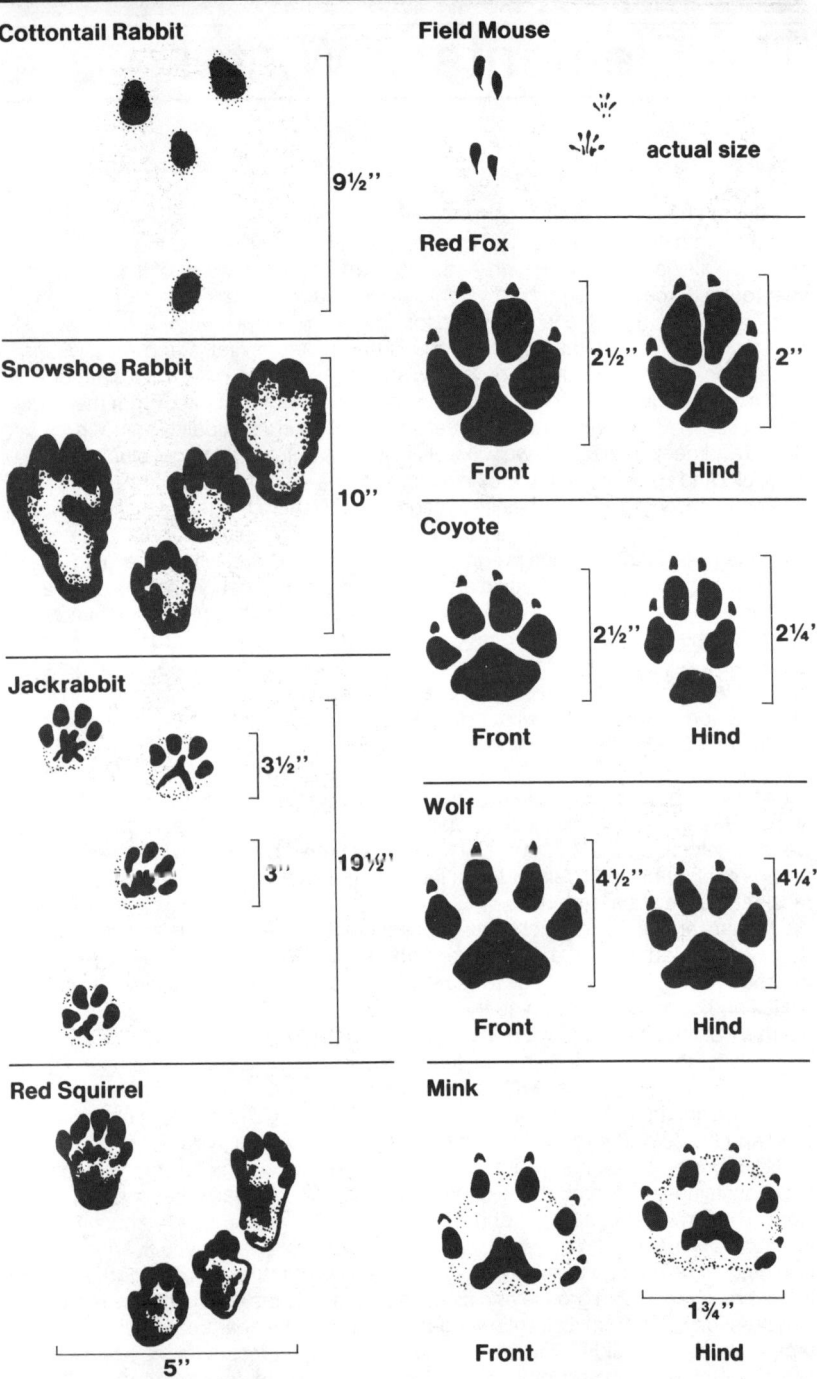

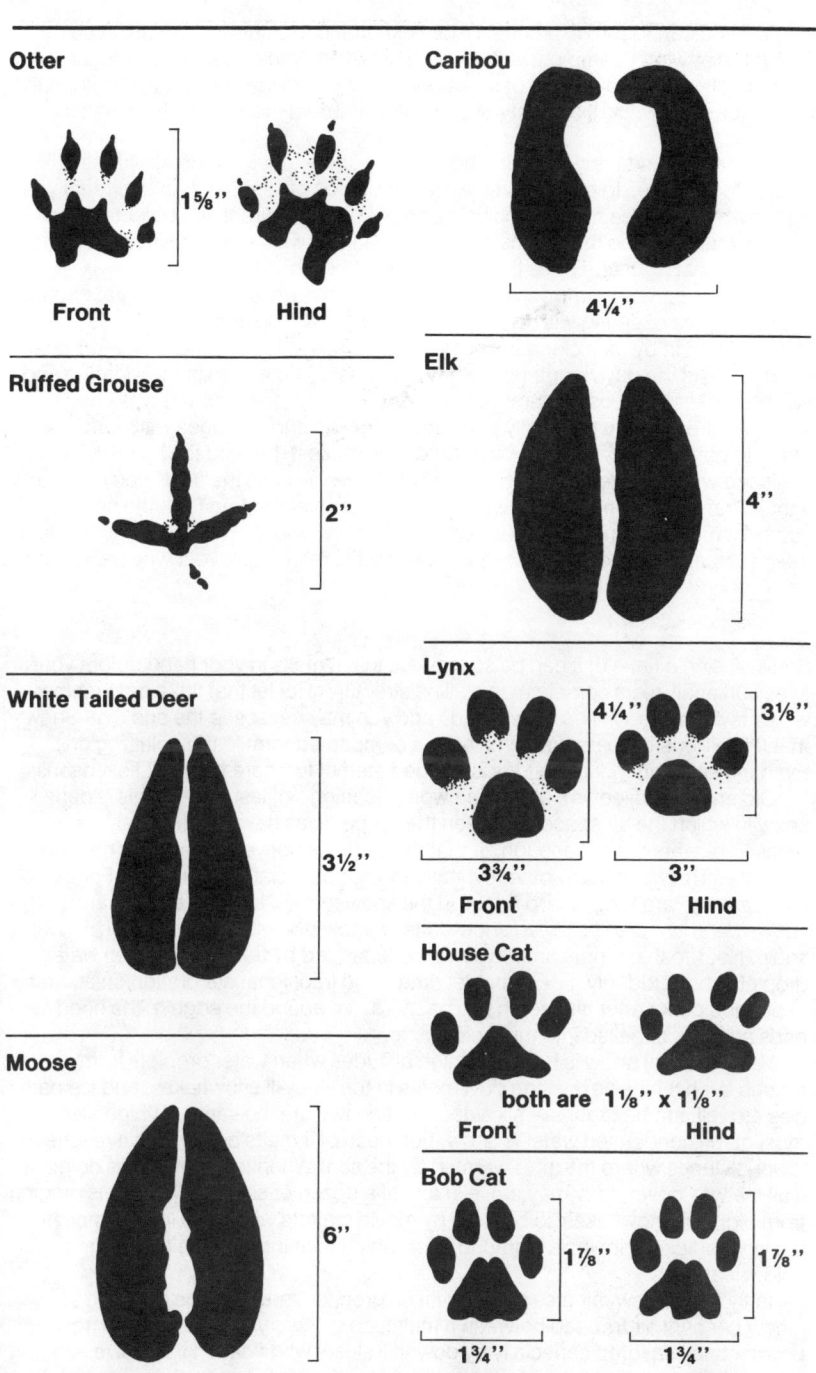

sions. If you can round up a couple more experienced skiers, you might even try your hand at winter camping, with a one-night outing for starters and a longer trek after that. It's also the season of races: everything from the Canadian Marathon to a local fun race present a variety of choices that would more than fill up the time you have free.

Late March and early April are the seasons of the tubes. There are tubes of sticky klister waxes to grip the wet snows and tubes of suntan lotion to protect your winter-whitened face from the powerful combination of direct and reflected sun. If you are touring in the mountains you will come back with a face tan as dark as that of a Caribbean tourist. This is the season when the world begins to come alive. Animals are active in the woods and overhead crows are starting to migrate north, the harbingers of spring with their raucous calls. You hide under a pine tree and try to draw them in by mimicking their calls and are rewarded by a flurry of wing-beats overhead. As the days lengthen, the snow becomes pure corn in the morning and you are whizzing across nature's ball bearings. But by afternoon it has turned to slush. At streams you hesitantly poke the remaining snow bridges with your poles, trying to gauge if they will get you across. You make it, but find the bridge virtually vanished when you return that way two hours later. Across the fields you dash, a light jacket tied around your waist and sunglasses steamed up from the heat as you twist and turn among the bare patches. Finally, you unsnap the bindings for the last time, at the edge of a muddy road, and carefully pick your way back to the car.

Snow

Snow. A single flake of it can be so tenuous that it melts in your hand before your eyes can analyze its complex, crystalline structure. But let that flake get together with a few hundred trillion of its friends and you may never see the end of it. Snow that fell millions of years ago remains in a compacted form in the polar regions. Even the snow on mountain tops is dubbed eternal for more than poetic reasons.

Old snow is called firn, a German word meaning "of last year." This is dense snow in which the air spaces between the ice particles have been greatly compressed but there is still enough air that the stuff has not yet turned into the solid form: ice. There are many other evocative words associated with snow. For example, *sastrugi* are long, sharp ridges in the snow formed by wind erosion and snow, *barchan* are U-shaped snow drifts or snow dunes formed by fresh, blowing snow. Hoarfrost and rime are ice particles separated by trapped air when water droplets cool suddenly. For example, rime is the traditional decoration on an arctic explorer's parka after his breath has been frozen around the edge of the hood seconds after it is expelled into the frigid air.

We know that snow is formed at high altitudes when water droplets form around such things as passing dust motes in the sky. All snowflakes, and ice particles as well, are hexagonal– six sided– but no two are the same. At high altitudes most of the condensed water is snow, but much of it melts by the time it reaches lower altitudes where the air is warmed by the sun. When the snowflakes do make it all the way down, they may arrive in any of a dozen or so classified forms ranging from big, soft snowflakes so beloved by movie makers who try to imitate them to the tiny particles known as diamond dust, which float through the air on some cold, clear days.

In those first few minutes after arrival on ground, snow may be as much as ninety per cent air trapped between a multitude of ice crystals. This is the fresh powder snow favored especially by downhill skiers who float on its elusive substance. Within a short time, snow begins a process of metamorphism in which the fluffy flakes begin to change into rounded granules. The process is often called

In some areas dogs are trained to search for people buried by avalanches.

settling because the snow pack begins to lose air content and literally settles closer to the ground. Such exterior forces as wind or the passing of skis can greatly speed up the process. If the snow is at a high enough altitude or latitude, it will become firn and eventually may become ice as the air is displaced.

Insignificant in small numbers, snowflakes can take on awesome proportions as they add up. For example, twenty-five centimetres (ten inches) of snow will put as much as ten tons pressure on the roof of an average house and you may have to shovel a ton to clear your sidewalks and driveway after such a storm.

Avalanches – One of the most impressive forms in which a skier can ever encounter snow is as an avalanche. It is one of nature's greatest destructive forces, ranking right up there with the hurricane, earthquake and tidal wave. Avalanches have been recorded at speeds of 360 kilometres per hour (225 m.p.h.) or about twice the world speed record on skis. When a big slide comes down, everything moves: century-old trees, boulders as big as houses, houses themselves, churches, schools, trains and any other structures not specially designed to let the snow roll over them smoothly. The forces are known to exceed 100 tons per square metre. Snow slides have their worst record in well inhabited alpine regions, particularly Europe and now the West, as more and more people settle and ski there. But even Easterners might look at snowslopes with more respect if they remembered two Scarborough (metropolitan Toronto) girls killed in a slide on a twenty-metre (seventy-five foot) long toboggan slope and a skier at Blue Mountain who had to wait for hours until he was rescued by friends from a relatively small slide on a little used trail.

Much is known about avalanches and the fact that they result from any of a series of factors influencing fallen snow, including degree of slope, sun, wind, sound and movement of such things as skis. Most important of all is the snow structure itself. Fresh, fluffy snow can slide quite readily because of its own instability on a slope and often does during a storm, but once it settles for a few hours the arts and science of predicting avalanches get much trickier.

Snow can be affected by a process called sublimation, in which the ice crystals at the extremities of a snowflake vaporize and then re-freeze nearer the centre of the crystal. This is destructive metamorphism. Then these granules can undergo constructive metamorphism in which they literally grow cup crystals a centimetre long. The crystals form a highly unstable layer beneath the even, white surface which the skier sees before him. In effect, they create a sub-surface of ball bearings beneath an expanse of snow and it may take no more than the bark of a dog, a puff of wind, a few more seconds of sunshine or the movement of a skier to break the tenuous bond and send tons of snow sliding downhill.

Experts have spent years trying to find ways to forecast and prevent avalanches, but Fred Schleiss, the avalanche analyst who decides when traffic can safely move through the Rogers Pass in British Columbia, says much is still unknown. He says even the experts work on sixty per cent technology and forty per cent art.

Peter Scharer of Vancouver, an avalanche expert with the National Research Council, says part of the expertise in predicting avalanches is simply gut feeling and that is what makes a good mountain guide. The researchers have their "snow plots" where they can slice away at the snow pack every day and look at the crystal formation. The guide goes by his training and experience with certain slopes and weather conditions. He will try to confirm his suspicions by jabbing an inverted ski pole into the snow, looking for an unstable layer below. He may even take a calculated risk and try to guess where the shear line or upper limit of an avalanche would be, then stamp his skis there to see if he can trigger a small slide. It is a demanding task and even guides get hurt once in a while.

For the cross-country skier going into potential avalanche terrain, and basically that does mean the West, ignorance imposes a high risk. The safest measure is to hire a qualified guide who knows the area. The next best – and a distant second for people unfamiliar with mountains – is to check with experts such as National Parks Service snow specialists in the area. They know the usual avalanche patterns for an area and often can warn you of particular hazards in a given area. As well, they may be able to map out a safe route for your party.

You should regard any slope steeper than fifteen degrees as having some avalanche potential and treat it with at least some respect. This respect should increase after heavy snowfalls or rains which can make conditions suddenly unstable. Most cross-country skiers will be travelling the flatter mountain valleys and won't run the same risk as alpine oriented touring parties, but even so they should watch out for hazards. When an avalanche sweeps down a slope it often keeps going right into the valley and can hurl shattered trees and debris more than a kilometre across the valley bottom.

If you are travelling in avalanche country, there are some precautions to take and things to keep in mind when you are near slopes. One of the simplest protections you can carry is fifteen metres (fifty feet) of brightly colored nylon cord known as avalanche cord. When you are skiing on a slope you think could avalanche, let the cord run freely behind on the principle that if you are buried there is a good chance a piece of nylon will remain on the surface and direct rescuers to you. As in many wilderness skiing situations, you should remove your pole straps; in this case, it is so you can cover your face in a hurry if the choking powder snow flies up or so you can make swimming motions as you try to stay near the surface.

A well equipped party will carry avalanche probes and shovels for locating and digging out anyone trapped by sliding snow. The most expensive ($100 plus) and one of the most effective protections are the small radio transmitter-receivers sold under such names as Skadi and Pieps and used by helicopter ski parties which are constantly in avalanche country. All members of a group carry one tucked underneath their clothing and set to transmit a beeping radio signal. If one person is buried, the other members switch to "receive" and use their sets as radio locators.

Of course the best route in avalanche country is around any area that looks as if it could slide, but this will inevitably become a question of judgement and you will feel pressed by falling night, an empty stomach and other factors. If you are crossing a slope with a possible hazard, each member of the group should go separately and the others should watch carefully. In case one skier is buried, the others should keep watching, then start digging and probing in the area below where the person was last seen. Form a straight line and probe with the tails of skis if necessary. At the same time don't forget there could be a second avalanche, so you should keep an eye peeled above.

If it is you who are caught in a slide take hope and remember the words of Fred Schleiss: "There's no slide I've triggered that's outpaced me in the first five seconds." In other words, if you are near the edge of the avalanche there is a chance you can ski down and to one side enough to escape all or most of its effects. In any case, try to stay on your feet and if the snow is already moving around you, dig your poles in uphill and try to hang on. If you go under, keep your hands near your face and try to remember to cover your face with one hand and reach straight up with the other. The most important thing is to cover your face, then quickly scratch out as much of a breathing space as possible. People have survived as long as ten days buried in avalanches, but have also suffocated in a few minutes if the snow seeped into their mouths or formed a solid mass around their heads.

All that is not to terrorize people from ever going within a mile of a mountain but rather to instill a certain respect and awareness of avalanches. Once aware, you stand a far better chance of being alert and learning more about the subject.

Ice

All snow is ice and air and if given enough time will become solid ice as air pockets between ice particles disappear. Given certain conditions, such as very high wind, this may happen almost instantly. Mountaineers at high altitudes have found that gale-force winds will pack the snow so hard that it virtually becomes ice in seconds and has to be chopped away from equipment with an ice axe.

The cross-country skier is more likely to find ice beneath his skis as the result of other skiers packing a trail. As each ski passes over the snow, it briefly melts the surface with friction and leaves a microscopic trail of water which immediately refreezes. In addition, it packs the snow and speeds up the process of sublimation which also leads to ice formation.

Most back-country skiers will also run across ice in the form of frozen lakes, rivers and streams and will probably use the flat, snow-covered surface as a place to pick up a bit of time on a long trip. It is worth remembering that a smooth surface, like the even surface of a slope before it avalanches, can be deceptive.

The times of greatest hazard, of course, are in the fall freeze-up and during the spring melt, but few ice surfaces can automatically be considered completely safe at any time. In the middle of winter a fast current will be nibbling at the underside of the ice on a river and may leave only a shell of snow on the top. Lakes are sometimes fed by streams which pump a steady flow of water to one area and create a thin spot in the ice. Narrows between two lakes or in the course of a river are notorious for having weak spots where the current is a bit faster and have claimed many a snowmobile, passengers and all.

Experienced travellers will check the ice conditions with residents of the area if possible, and will find out something of the weather patterns just before the trip. As they travel, they will make frequent stabbing checks of the surface ahead with the tips of their ski poles. Sometimes a pole will penetrate the snow and turn up slush beneath. This bears further checking. Is it just a layer of water atop the solid ice or is the ice below unsound? If for some reason you absolutely have to cross ice that appears rotten, you may be better off to carry a stout sapling, as long as you are tall and hold it crosswise. If you go through, the pole will probably hold on either side and prevent you going right under. Another good precaution is to rope up all members of a party.

A complete dunking far from shelter can be disastrous, but even a wet foot can pose a severe threat of freezing. One reaction taken by some northern dwellers when they put a foot through the ice is to immediately plunge it into soft, dry snow. The snow, if full of air spaces, will act somewhat as a blotter and can absorb part of the moisture. This is another reason to carry a change of socks in your pack: they could save you from a frostbitten foot. Once badly wet it becomes a matter of judgment. If the weather is not too frigid and you are not too far from shelter, it may be worthwhile to make a dash for camp or car. All members of the party should contribute some warm clothing, especially that in the packs and strip off all the wet clothing possible from the victim. Then set out at top speed and keep an eye on the wet person for signs of frostbite. The alternative is to immediately make an emergency camp and start a roaring fire. There will be a time consuming wait while you carefully dry out his clothing without burning it up.

Weather

Wind, cloud, sun and temperature all govern the lives we lead, especially if we are spending them out of doors. They are part of the weather patterns which dictate whether or not we will be able to ski, and if so, what the conditions will be like.

Fallible as they are, the weather reports from government meteorologists are still the best indicators most of us can find to get at least a general idea of the weather for our area. These reports tend to paint the picture in broad brush strokes and will tell you if a warming trend is in the air or if cold weather will continue. They can also forecast major storm fronts and alert you to possible hazards. Sometimes it takes a bit of research to get the report for the area you plan to ski. Some radio stations, particularly CBC, will occasionally carry forecasts for a wide area beyond the city where the station is based. Sometimes there is a government weather station you can phone for up-to-the-minute information on specific localities.

Sometimes weather reports are not available and in areas such as mountain country, they may be of little specific use. Within a given weather system there are frequent local variations: in the mountains you may have sun in one valley and a storm in the next, and lakeshores often have more cloud than areas a few kilometres inland. Winter weather can have a drastic effect on your skiing, especially if you are going off the beaten track. If a severe storm is brewing, you probably wouldn't want to stray more than a couple of kilometres from the base and certainly wouldn't risk heading out for a day or two of winter camping. If the weather has been steadily warming, you would seriously reconsider any trip into the mountains where wet snow could double the time of travel and increase the avalanche hazard.

Every skier should develop a bit of weather sense to augment forecasts that may be already outdated by sudden changes or may not be valid for a specific area. Just as you learn to gauge the type of snow before applying wax in the morn-

The first part of making camp in deep snow is creating a solid platform for the tent. This means stamping down the snow with your boots until it becomes as hard as earth.

ing, you should learn to scan the sky for cloud signs. There are plenty of standby signs for bad weather: rising wind, sharp changes in temperature and build-up of clouds. However, strong winds in one area or under certain conditions may mean different things. In one part of the country they could be the sign of an impending storm and in another area they may be a sign that the weather is clearing. Or they may occur before, during and after a storm.

Forecasting local weather is best learned by observation and experience, but many useful tips can be gleaned from true experts such as guides and rangers who live and work outdoors and are used to keeping a weather eye for their own safety and comfort. Many mountain guides carry a pocket altimeter, which is just a barometer with the dial working in reverse. In other words, a rising altimeter (if you are stationary) means a falling barometer and the probability of bad weather.

Temperature – Most of us are constantly curious about the temperature around us and for skiers the concern is even more justified. Certainly this, along with the condition of the snow surface, dictates what kind of wax we should begin with on any day and the kind of clothing we will wear and pack. The temperature may also affect the choice of route. A sheltered route among the trees would be more appropriate on a cold, windy day. If the temperature is rising and there is a possibility of precipitation, we might also pack rain gear as a precaution against a shower. When the wind is picking up, the temperature is dropping as a result of the wind chill factor. For example, the air temperature according to your pocket thermometer could be five degrees C (forty degrees F) but with a sixty kilometre (forty m.p.h.) wind your exposed flesh would feel a temperature of minus eleven degrees C or ten degrees F.

On a minus twenty degrees C day with a fresh breeze, there will be danger of exposed skin freezing in as little as one minute and you should take great care to cover even your face with a scarf or mask. In truly extreme cold, such as is rarely found in the lower latitudes of Canada, not only the outer skin but the lining of the lungs could suffer damage. When the temperature starts getting into the minus forty degree C range, you should use caution about moving quickly and drawing in great breaths of air.

The other side of the coin or the clouds as the case may be is the warmth from the sun. This is the life-giving force which powers our world and creates our weather as it evaporates the water which makes the clouds which make the rain and the snow we ski on. From December through January it seems to vanish from the sky and in the high North it is almost completely absent, creating a period when people can work and move about for only brief periods without artificial light, heat and insulation. The legendary resistance of the Eskimo to deep cold is largely a result of his knack for staying out of the cold and beneath a warm layer of fur and insulating snow as much as possible during the deep winter.

For many centuries man, particularly in northern latitudes, has respected and even worshiped the cycles of the sun as it drew further away from his land, then slowly started its trek back across the sky, melting the snow and warming upturned faces. Despite the artificial environments we create in an attempt to ignore winter, Canadians are still affected by the changes and, like other peoples, celebrate the return of Old Sol. Since the distant past, Europeans have marked the lengthening of the days in January and February with celebrations such as the famous Fasching of Germany. These celebrations have been transplanted to the New World and take such forms as the carnival in Rio, the Mardi Gras of New Orleans and the *Carnaval d'Hiver* (Winter Carnival) of Quebec City. In recent years the winter carnival has become a new part of life in many towns and cities across Canada, as people relax and let their hair down after a couple of months of cold and snow. For many skiers it is a time not only of celebration but competition – both serious and friendly – as people race for trophies and personal satisfaction. Many carnivals have cross-country races as part of their programs and draw both the trained competitors and erstwhile spectators who decide to try their newly developed skills in a run of a few kilometres with their neighbors.

Winter Photography

Photographs provide some of the best souvenirs of any trip, especially a tour through winter wonderlands of snow-clad trees, soft drifts and sun-sparkled snow. Winter photography is not quite as easy as snapping a family photo in the back yard. The extra equipment to carry all day can prove a bit cumbersome until you find a good place to stow it and picture taking can get tricky when you are trying to get a good shot of friends as they move quickly along a winding forest trail while you are fumbling with gloves and the focusing ring of your lens. However, even a passably good snapshot is worth the effort since it will provide a clear memory of that favorite trip for years to come.

Almost annual technological improvements in photo equipment make the preservation of those memories ever easier. One has to admire the photographs taken during the period up to the 1950s. Professionals and many ambitious amateurs lugged anywhere from ten to thirty pounds and more of view cameras, lenses, tripods and film in metal cases in addition to their skis and winter camping gear. They took few action shots with those cumbersome cameras but endurance and patience has rewarded them and us with some stunning winter scenes.

Now it is no longer necessary to pack a case of heavy equipment and freeze fingers in the recording of your exploits on skis. Even professionals rely on fine-grain film in highly portable thirty-five mm cameras. Most amateurs use this size film and many persons are satisfied with the results of the 110 "pocket camera" snapshots.

The technological squeeze play has produced some marvellous results for the wilderness traveller. Designers are steadily reducing the size of viewfinder style thirty-five mm cameras and many of them now fit comfortably under a ski jacket let alone in a belt pack or rucksack. One of the better models is the Konica Auto S-3 which allows the photographer to control the speed of the shutter manually and to override the automatic aperature very simply in order to obtain special effects or compensate for uneven lighting.

Most of the viewfinder cameras sold these days have lenses in the thirty-five to fifty mm range, which provide anything from a moderate wide-angle to a "normal" view of the subject. For more specialized shots, such as wide or extreme wide angles or for telephoto shots you are almost obliged to have a single lens reflex camera. This is a bulkier camera, more suitable to packing in a rucksack or carrying under the ski jacket for limited periods, but it provides the greatest flexibility in composition of photos and an unlimited (except financially) choice of lenses. You can slip on a fisheye lens to produce a splendid panorama of mountain tops or a 500 mm telephoto for nature photography.

One of the advantages of winter photography is the great reflecting surface of the snow. On sunny days in particular the light can be so strong, that a fast film – one with an ASA rating in the hundreds – will be overexposed at all but the highest shutter speed and tiniest aperture. This means that you can switch to slower, finer-grained films which in turn can be enlarged to great degrees without extreme loss of sharpness.

On the other hand you have to be careful with exposure to avoid the extremes of contrast that come with very bright light on a combination of white and dark surfaces. You almost need one exposure to get the nuances of light and shadow on the surface of the snow and another to bring out the details of clothing and

With a little luck or some skill in tracking a skier may find deer taking shelter or browsing in the woods. This western Mule deer is poised for a quick escape from such an intrusion.

equipment. If the skiers are in the distance and won't be seen in detail on the final print you will usually settle on an exposure weighted in favor of the snow, but if the skiers are close you may want to take a separate light meter reading on their faces. This is where a camera that can be manually controlled is useful.

High contrast can be used for dramatic effects. For example, shooting skiers backlit by the sun will produce sharp silhouettes. Another trick is to set the camera for a high shutter speed and the smallest aperture, then shoot to include the sun in the picture. The result will be a star image as the lens creates a controlled flare of light. At times you may want to add yellow, orange or even red filters when shooting with black and white film to increase contrast and bring out the texture of tree bark, mountain rock or wind-blown snow. The best way to get the desired effect is to have a bit of experience so it is worth shooting and processing a roll of film with different exposures before setting out on a trip you want well recorded.

While it is sometimes tempting to think of a Canadian winter only in terms of light and dark, there is plenty of color to provide memorable slide shows. Modern ski fashions produce groups of skiers garbed in all hues of the rainbow. Color film is also a good way to record that springtime tan. In addition to the colors of skiers, nature provides a range of greens in its spruce, balsam, fir and pine, the blue of snow in the shade of early morning or late afternoon and the blaze of orange and yellow from the rising and setting sun. Look for such color combinations as old wood set against a white snowfield, the gold of weeds against fresh snow in the early winter, reflections in open water and of course the blue of a clear winter sky as a backdrop for any panorama.

A word of caution about handling film and equipment in winter. Even with modern chemicals and lubricants delicate mechanisms can be slowed or even solidified by extremes of cold and film can become brittle enough to break if handled roughly. It is a good policy to sling a camera under the ski jacket, either beneath an arm or in front, to warm things up before shooting. This will help ensure the shutter is giving the exposure indicated and that the film will not be damaged during a rapid winding.

Car and Skier

Aside from a well-waxed pair of skis, your major method of transportation in the winter will likely be a car. If you are dedicated to searching out wilderness areas you may invest in something with four-wheel-drive, four big snow tires and lots of cargo space. Another variation on the travel theme is the camper van which has plenty of road clearance and provides overnight shelter if you have lots of insulation. However, most of us choose our vehicles for urban and highway driving and that means something that will cruise a freeway with respectable speed and at least moderate comfort. If we make regular ski trips in winter (and probably canoeing or camping trips in summer) we look for a car or station wagon with reasonable road clearance and cargo space and at least decent handling so it won't misbehave on icy or gravelled roads.

From there on it is a question of equipping the basic vehicle so you can cope with most winter driving situations. The number one priority is good snow tires. You may already have radial tires with an all-weather tread, which is suitable for light snow but not the heavy stuff. If you are doing a lot of driving in the country you should consider not only putting snow tires on the rear but on the front as well to improve the steering on snowy surfaces. In any case, you should carry a set of chains, one of the most useful emergency devices ever known to someone stuck in a snowbank. While full chains are ideal and may be necessary for some parts of the country, the type with two sets of links and a leather strap are effective enough for most situations where you are caught on a patch of ice or a small snowbank.

Of course a snow shovel is another very high priority. If space is at a premium in your car, a folding trench shovel will do most jobs in a little more time. Another effective tool for getting unstuck is a tow cable and this can be a lightweight nylon rope which takes little storage space. For those of us who get caught with a flat battery, and it happens to just about everyone sooner or later, a pair of jumper cables and instructions on how to use them are an investment which will be recouped on the first usage.

At any time of the year you may need a flashlight with fresh batteries and a set of road flares in case of a breakdown in a hazardous spot. If you are going to be messing around looking for things under the car you should have a pair of cotton work gloves and a plastic bag or two as at least minimal protection against dirt and grease. Cloths are also useful, particularly in winter when everything seems to be getting covered with fog or grime. It is handy to have one for wiping the salt spray off windows and lights and a clean cloth for wiping off the inside of fogged windows.

On the liquid side you should keep the windshield washer tank topped up with full-strength fluid from the pre-mixed jugs and should have a reasonably full jug in the car at all times for refilling the tank. On a wet and salty highway this can be almost as important as gasoline. Still on the fluids, you should have a tube of lock de-icer. If your car does not have a rear window de-fogger consider one of the kits now on the market or the cheap and effective frost shields which have been used for decades. Somewhere in the trunk of the car there should be at least a minimal tool kit, containing such things as a screwdriver, pliers, open end wrench, some electrical tape and some wire. If your car is very hard to start you might throw in a can of gas line de-icer and even one of starting fluid which is sprayed into the carburetor.

Long winter drives under poor visibility conditions tax the eyes. You might consider a set of quartz headlights a good investment for the extra visibility they offer, especially under adverse conditions.

In the ski carrying department, anyone with a valuable pair of skis and plans to park on a street for longer than a couple of minutes should look at a rack with locks. Most people discover sooner or later, but in case you hadn't noticed the correct way to carry skis is with the tips to the rear of the car. With road salt and sand an almost constant fact of winter life, no skier should carry equipment unprotected on the roof. In the first place the salt spray messes up any wax job you have started and moreover it will corrode the bindings. For those who have the flat style of roof racks there are now nylon ski envelopes which are light and waterproof.

If you are setting out on a long trip, especially on a nice day, you may not have heavy clothing but if you are planning a long trip, particularly one which will last into the night, you should have a pair of heavy boots and a warm jacket, hat and gloves in the car. Travellers in the north are usually advised to also carry a warm sleeping bag so they can hole up in the car until help arrives. One last warning, oft repeated but oft ignored. If the motor is running on a parked car keep a window open so carbon monoxide can't build up and suddenly knock you out.

Trails

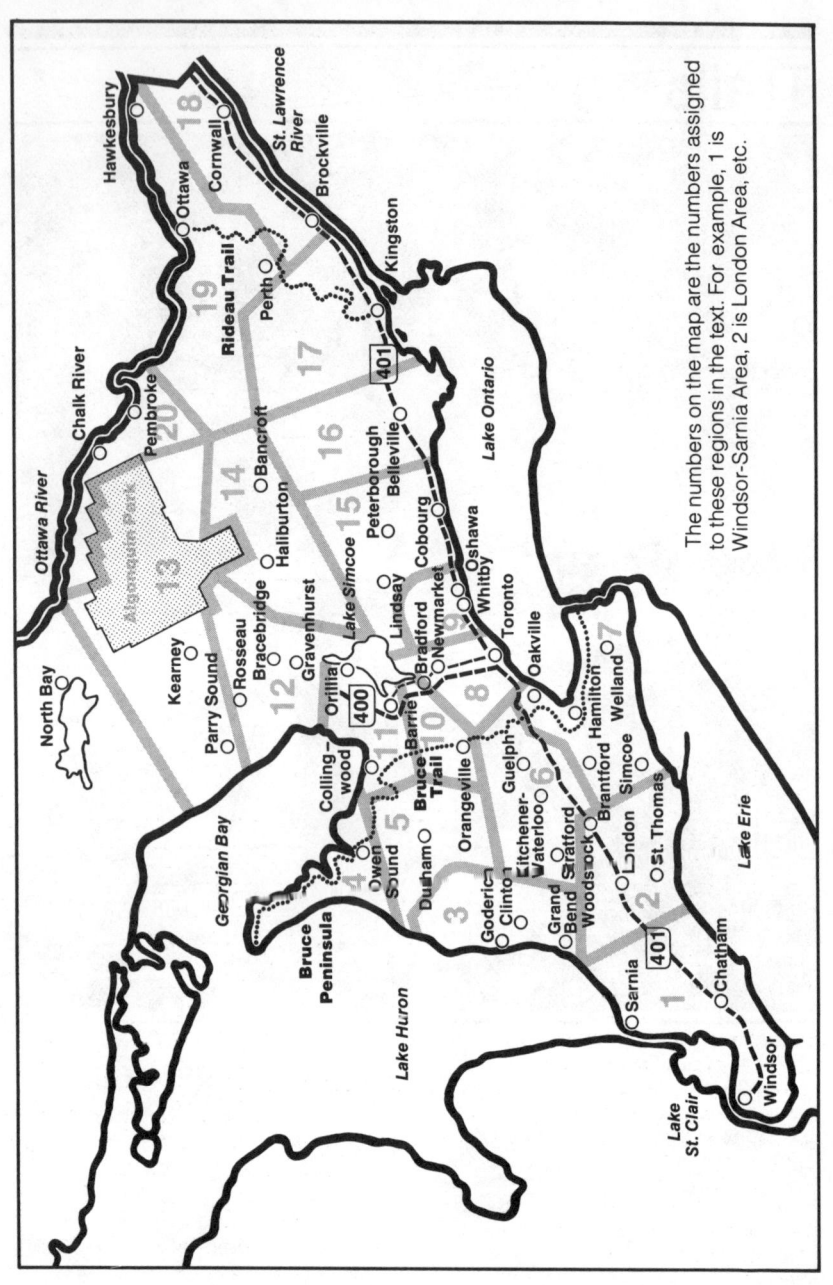

Southern Ontario Trails

Metric measurements have been used in the Trails section (km = kilometre, ha = hectare.) A metric conversion table appears on page 111.

1 Windsor – Sarnia Area

A.W. Campbell Conservation Area
LOCATION: From just north of Alvinston on Hwy. 79, go east 2 km on access road.
LENGTH: Just over 1 km.

Skiers can follow a walking trail on a 125 ha park along Sydenham R. Historic site, campground, picnic tables, interpretive centre, snowmobiling in area.

Devonwood Conservation Area
LOCATION: Windsor. Off Division Rd. just north of Cabana Rd.
LENGTH: About 3 km loop.

Trail is located in part of 36 ha conservation area. Terrain is flat and forested. Parking.

Maidstone Conservation Area
LOCATION: East of Windsor. From Essex north 4 km on County Rd. 25 to Puce.
LENGTH: About 1.5 km loop.

Winding trail is in Maidstone Township Central Conservation Area, 14 ha of flat, forested terrain. Area has parking, privies, information kiosk, reforestation area and demonstration windbreak. Brochures available at area.

Point Pelee National Park
LOCATION: From Leamington south 10 km.
LENGTH: 12 km of ski, bicycle and hiking trails plus 13 km of skiing on beaches.

Canada's most southerly peninsula is well known as a nature reserve and is famous as a stopping point for migratory birds. In recent years park staff have been breaking trails and offering guided tours for cross-country skiers. There are two specific ski trails plus hiking and biking trails and the beach areas, all dependent on snow cover in this Canadian banana belt. There is always a possibility of seeing deer, rabbits, pheasants, owls and other wildlife. Skating on cleared ice areas. Maps and more detailed information available at the park's interpretive centre or by writing: Point Pelee National Park, RR 1, Leamington, Ont. N8H 3V4.

Rondeau Provincial Park
LOCATION: From Chatham 40 km south on Hwys. 40, 3 and 51.
LENGTH: 16 km of marked trails.

Any part of Rondeau Park is "fair game" for the cross-country skier. Since snow conditions are often very limited, it would be best to inquire at the park office in order to locate the best skiing opportunity. Rondeau is a flat sandspit formation on Lake Erie shoreline that is heavily wooded by rare vegetation types. Roads and walking trails wind through an immense hardwood forest, the largest remaining forest in Southwestern Ontario.

Skiers should be careful about venturing onto Rondeau Bay in the wintertime. The bay does partly freeze over but is generally unsafe for winter activities. Many species of birds, wildlife and rare vegetation are found at the park. An interpretive program has been established to aid the visitor in discovering more about some of Rondeau's unique features. A campground with a limited number of electrical sites is operated in the winter with heated washrooms, trailer dumping facilities, etc. Hotels are located within 16 km of the park. For information contact the Park Superintendant, Rondeau Provincial Park, RR 1, Morpeth, Ont.

2 London Area

Parkhill
LOCATION: Near village of Parkhill near L. Huron shoreline in Western Ontario.

There is skiing on 754 ha of parkland, with about 6 km of trails at Parkhill Conservation area east of village and on the Saddler Tract, 5 km west of the village on Hwy. 7.

Circle R Ranch Touring Centre
LOCATION: Off Hwy. 2 in Delaware, west of London.

LENGTH: 18 km.
The centre has five loop trails ranging from a 1.3 km beginner run to the 5 km Tuckerman expert trail. All trails fan out from the lodge. Rolling terrain, wooded in the Dingman Creek valley. The area, which is an outdoor education centre and children's camp during the summer, has ski instruction and rentals during winter weekends and holidays. There is also a floodlit area for evening lessons during the week. Trails groomed and tracked. Cafeteria, fireplaces, and waxing area in lodge. Sleigh rides. Maps available at lodge. Site of Forest City Loppet, which includes races and a tour held each February. For more information write: Circle R Ranch, Box 85, Delaware, Ont. or phone (519) 471-3799.

Longwoods Road Conservation Area
LOCATION: From London west 26 km on Hwy. 2. Proceed on Hwy. 2 about 3.2 km west of village of Delaware and follow signs.
LENGTH: About 11 km.
Both wooded and open areas. Some steep trails. Suitable for beginners and intermediate skiers. Trail passes by Ska Nah Doht Indian Village, reconstructed Neutral Indian Village. The area has a wide range of small wildlife and good scenery. Accommodation in London. Maps available by writing to: Lower Thames Valley Conservation Authority, 41 Fourth St., Chatham, Ont.

Coldstream Conservation Area
LOCATION: From London west 24 km on Hwy. 22 to Poplar Hill then north 1.6 km on county road.
LENGTH: About 1 km.
This ski trail follows a nature trail through forest, marsh and some open areas in a 50 ha park. Historic site, campground and picnic tables. Located on Sydenham R.

Thames Valley Trail
LOCATION: Trail begins at Byron Bridge in London's Springbank Park and runs upstream along the Thames R. to the town of St. Marys.
LENGTH: Full distance is 62 km but there is 20 km loop running to Fanshawe L. and back.
This is basically a hiking trail. Some sections are on city streets and are not suitable for skiing. In country the trail runs along the river valley with some steep sections along hillsides and some fence crossovers using stiles. Snow conditions can vary widely. There is no trail grooming. Much of the trail is on private land and users are asked to respect that fact. Trail is marked with arrowhead blazes. The trail is maintained by the Thames Valley Trail Assn., 403 Lansing Ave., London, Ont. N6K 2J2. Maps and membership applications available.

Fanshawe Conservation Area
LOCATION: East edge of London. At Fanshawe L. on Thames R. On east side of Clarke Rd.
This 360 ha park includes the river, small lake and a section of the Thames Valley Trail. This hiking-ski trail provides the only marked route, but there are many areas for skiers to make their own trails in wooded and open areas. Rentals, lessons, shelter. Fanshawe Pioneer Village at the area. For more information contact the Upper Thames River Conservation Authority, Box 6278, Station D, London, Ont. N5V 2Y8 or phone (519) 451-2800.

George White Memorial Outdoor Centre
LOCATION: London. On west side of Clarke Rd. N., about 200 m north of Thames R. bridge.
LENGTH: 8 km in four loops of 1-3 km.
The centre, owned by the London YM-YWCA, is on 32 ha of flood plain and upland area with 1.5 km along the river. Trails are on both types of land. More than sixteen habitat types have been identified including: cat-tail marsh, cedar swamp, scrub meadow, hardwood forest and coniferous forest. Nature programs are run throughout the year. Trails groomed, rentals, instruction available, skating on one-acre pond. Open weekends and evenings by appointment for groups. Maps, nature guides and accommodation from London YM-YWCA, 433 Wellington St., London, Ont. N6A 3P7 or phone (519) 432-3706.

Fisher Conservation Area
LOCATION: From Port Ryerse in Long Point region west 6 km on Hwy. 24 to Fisher's Glen.
This is a 49 ha conservation area on the L. Erie shoreline. Some cross-country trails.

Long Point Region Conservation Authority
Conservation Authority officials say there are extensive skiing possibilities on about 4000 ha of land scattered over two dozen

areas. The authority has marked no trails and charges no winter fees but reports that some private groups have marked trails. In addition, there are many kilometres of fire roads, nature trails and other paths which are suitable for skiing. Much of the country is gently rolling and forested. A compass is recommended in the larger woodlots. For a brochure locating the various areas write: Long Point Region Conservation Authority, Box 525, Simcoe, Ont. N3Y 4N5. Send self-addressed stamped envelope. A 51 by 76 cm wall map is also available for $2.50.

Iroquois Beach Provincial Park

LOCATION: Western edge of Port Burwell on County Road 39.

This 224 ha park on the L. Erie shoreline is used for cross-country skiing. Snowmobiling allowed on park roads.

Trillium Woods Provincial Nature Reserve

LOCATION: Southwest of Woodstock. From Sweaburg exit on Hwy. 401, follow County Rd. 12 south of Sweaburg. Continue 1.6 km to first intersection beyond village and turn right for 8 km.
LENGTH: 1 km.

10 ha of wooded, gently rolling terrain known for trilliums in the spring. For accommodation, contact Chamber of Commerce, Woodstock.

Vansittart Woods Wildlife Management Area

LOCATION: Oxford Outdoor Education Centre on northeastern outskirts of Woodstock.
LENGTH: 1 km.

96 ha of gentle to rolling terrain with low-lying swampy areas. Trail goes through pine plantations, mixed hardwood forest. For accommodation, contact Chamber of Commerce, Woodstock.

Woodstock Ski Club

LOCATION: From Woodstock northwest 11 km via Hwy. 59.
LENGTH: About 17 km.

Cross-country and downhill area. Cross-country trails begin at club and run east and west in a series of loops. Terrain has some hills and cover varies from open to cedar woods. Wildlife include deer, small animals and birds. Picnic areas, warm-up hut. Trails marked and map available on site. Special suppers and moonlight outings with hot snack on the trail.

3 Goderich Area

Benmiller Inn

LOCATION: Village of Benmiller, between Goderich and Clinton. Inn is on County Rd. 1, just north of Hwy. 8.
LENGTH: About 60 km in four loop trails of 15 to 20 km.

Benmiller Inn maintains a series of trails over private property and there are adjacent trails in the Maitland Falls Conservation Area. Terrain varies from open farmland to partly wooded areas with small hills. Food, drink and accommodation at Benmiller Inn and guest house accommodation at Cherrydale Farm. Outdoor skating rink, heated indoor pool, whirlpool, sauna, track, etc. for guests. For information and maps contact Benmiller Inn, Benmiller, RR 4, Goderich, Ont. N7A 3Y1.

Hullet Wildlife Management Area

LOCATION: From Clinton northeast 6 km on Hwy. 4.

This is a 1840 ha parkland area in Western Ontario countryside with some trails.

Pinery Provincial Park

LOCATION: From Grand Bend south 8 km on Hwy. 21.
LENGTH: Trail network of over 20 km with loops and individual circuits for different levels of expertise.

The full trail traverses the entire topographic range of Pinery's 2400 ha of natural environment park. Pinery's dune topography offers many "ups and downs" for the cross-country skier through close pine and oak forested areas. Downhill ski run on weekends. Heated chalet, tobogganing, skating rink, 130 electrical outlets at campsites, heated washrooms and refreshment facilities. Pinery Park is one of the largest provincial parks in the southern part of Ontario and offers possibilities for all types of winter recreation.

4 Bruce Peninsula

The Bruce Trail

LOCATION: From Queenston, on Niagara R., north to Tobermory at the tip of the Bruce Peninsula.
LENGTH: About 700 km.

The Bruce is the mother lode of hiking in Ontario and one of Canada's major trails.

Much of it traverses rolling farm and woodlands typical of Southern Ontario and is very suitable for cross-country skiing. As this 1.5 metre wide footpath winds across the landscape, it traverses some of the most scenic parts of this region. In many places it crosses or passes close to ski resorts or public parklands with cross-country trails and is commonly adopted into trail networks. For example, it passes the major ski resort developments in the Collingwood - Thornbury belt and in the Beaver Valley.

Though much of trail is skiable, anyone planning an outing would be wise to do some research on the terrain crossed before setting out. Parts of the trail pass through some of the wildest and most rugged countryside in Southern Ontario and are either unskiable or suitable only for experts. Unless you know or get direct knowledge of the suitability of any section, it would be wise to obtain a copy of *The Bruce Trail Guide Book,* which has text and topographical maps of the entire route.

The trail is generally easy to follow, using the white blazes painted on trees. Side trails are marked in blue. The only problems might arise in areas, like the Bruce Peninsula, where blazes are painted on rocks and might be snow-covered. In any case, it is wise to carry a compass and topographic maps. The Bruce section, particularly near the tip, is extremely rugged as it passes along the edge of the escarpment and sometimes winds down the rocks to the shoreline. Anyone tackling an area like that should travel in a party with experienced skiers and get detailed information about the condition of the trail.

Geologically the trail passes over a variety of land. The escarpment is formed of dolomite limestone and the softer shale. In places, erosion over the millenia has left the harder dolomite overhanging the base of shale creating precipitous ledges and such unique formations as the freestanding "flowerpots." As well, the dolomite has split in many places, making fascinating caves.

The Bruce Trail was started in 1959 and finished in 1967. It is maintained by local clubs and largely traverses private land. For information write: Bruce Trail Assn., Box 857, Hamilton, Ont. L8N 3N9.

Cyprus Lake Provincial Park

LOCATION: About 10 km south of Tobermory at the tip of the Bruce Peninsula.

This 640 ha park runs northeast from near Hwy. 6 to the north shore of the Bruce Peninsula overlooking Georgian Bay. The Bruce Trail runs along the top of the Niagara Escarpment at this point and the trail club describes a section of just over one kilometre here as "beyond any doubt the most spectacular part of the entire (700 km) Bruce Trail." For example, it includes Overhanging Point, a precipice projecting several hundred metres high over the bay and many caves, at least one with an underwater connection to the bay. The Bruce here is at its wildest and most rugged and especially in the winter is a lonely and beautiful place.

Skiers wanting to explore the region can follow park roads to many areas without much trouble, but the Bruce Trail tends to be winding and rugged in many places. Care is obviously necessary along the high cliffs and around cave areas. Anyone wanting to bushwhack should carry a good pack of equipment, including climbing rope, compass and maps. This area is chopped by the edges of three topographic sheets of the 1:50,000 series, including Dorcas Bay, Dyer Bay and the west sheet of Flowerpot I. in the 41 H map region.

Skinner Bluffs Conservation Area

LOCATION: East of Wiarton overlooking Colpoy Bay. From hamlet of Lake Charles go north about 5 km on local road which crosses escarpment before heading toward North Keppel.

This is a highly scenic lookout and at places the limestone cliffs have been spectacularly eroded and are perilously overhanging the valley more than 30 m below. From places you can see White Cloud and Griffith Islands at the mouth of Colpoy Bay and you can look out over Georgian Bay. The Bruce Trail follows the Niagara Escarpment at this point, wandering through pasture and by farm fields before plunging into stands of tall maples. Conservation area of about 240 ha. Locating site is difficult and requires detailed maps such as Bruce County road map. Managed by Sauble Valley Conservation Authority, Box 759, RR 4, Owen Sound, Ont. N4K 5W9.

Rankin Ski Trails

LOCATION: Red Bay area north of Sauble Beach and west of Wiarton in Bruce Peninsula. Access points at western edge of Red L. and west side of road running south to Oliphant.

LENGTH: 17 km. Sections of 8 and 9 km with small loops.

Trails are located on scenic land owned privately and by the Sauble Valley Conservation Authority. They pass over largely forested, rolling countryside with some short, steep hills and ridges. Mature hardwood bush, small meadows, cedar swamp and small inland lakes. Trail runs from Spry L. in south to Beattie L. in north. Variety of winter birds and wildlife includes deer, rabbit, fox, skunk and the occasional brush wolf, which is extremely shy and rarely seen.

The 9 km northern section of the trail is more rugged and has some steep sections. A short side trip from this trail leads to Tower Hill, the highest point in the area, and gives a view of some of the finest scenery on the western edge of the peninsula. The 8 km southern section also has some steep pitches and areas where the trail wanders through heavy brush. A good afternoon outing would be the loop around North Hodgins L. Most areas demand intermediate ability. No camping, fires or motorized vehicles. Trails marked with red blazes. Compass useful.

For maps and brochures contact Sauble Valley Conservation Authority, Box 759, RR 4, Owen Sound, Ont. N4K 5W9. Accommodation at Red Bay Lodge, RR 1, Mar, Ont. N0H 1X0.

Sucker Creek Conservation Area

LOCATION: On the shore of L. Huron north of Sauble Beach. Located on Sucker Cr. between Pike Bay and Howdenvale.

This conservation property of about 120 ha is centred around a large creek and swamp area just inland from the rugged shoreline in a sparsely inhabited area. There is some snowmobiling and plenty of opportunity for bushwhacking on strong skis. Lakeshore area is beautiful, but on days when the wind sweeps across more than 100 km of open lake the skiing is warmer in the dense bush of deciduous and coniferous growth.

Keppel Escarpment Conservation Area

LOCATION: North of Owen Sound about 16 km. Follow County Roads 1 and 17 to cliffs of Niagara Escarpment.
LENGTH: 13 km.

Skiing is on a 1160 ha conservation area based on the Niagara Escarpment. Area is highly scenic with good views over surrounding countryside. The Bruce Trail passes through this region.

Harrison Park

LOCATION: In south end of Owen Sound off Second Ave. E.
LENGTH: 4 km.

This attractive park, located beside the Sydenham R., combines wooded hillsides and rolling lands along the river. Trails wind through both heavily and lightly wooded areas and there are opportunities for downhill runs between the trees for the more daring. A small downhill ski hill is located nearby and area is also used for tobogganing. Snack bar.

Inglis Falls Trail

LOCATION: Inglis Falls Conservation Area, 5 km south of Owen Sound on Inglis Falls Rd.
LENGTH: 4 km loop.

This short loop follows part of the Bruce Trail in a local beauty spot where the Sydenham River pours over the edge of the Niagara Escarpment. Trail is on mostly even terrain and is rated suitable for novice to intermediate skiers. The conservation area has 384 ha of parkland along the escarpment and river. Skiers can visit the remains of one of the earliest mill complexes in this part of the province. Park area includes some farmland, and bush of maple, beech, aspen, basswood, birch, poplar, hemlock and cedar. Area is open daily. Map available. For more information contact the North Grey Region Conservation Authority, Box 759, Owen Sound, Ont. N4K 5W9 or phone (519) 376-3076.

West Rocks

LOCATION: Owen Sound, atop west hill and on southern edge of development at Niagara Escarpment.

This conservation area is located on rugged cliff area and includes a section of the Bruce Trail. It is used by many local residents for short ski outings.

Bay Motor Inn Ski Village

LOCATION: South of Owen Sound. From Chatsworth south on Hwy. 10, then east and north on local roads following signs for about 5 km to entrance.
LENGTH: 5 km.

The Ski Village is a product of the Georgas brothers of Owen Sound, an active group of skiers who were among the first in the area to treat cross-country skiing seriously. Originally this resort was known mainly for downhill skiing and for jumping competitions, but cross-country skiing through the rolling countryside of fields and forests has developed in recent years. The area has a full range of facilities, including instruction, sales, rentals, food, liquor and lodging nearby. From this area skiers can link up with the Bruce Trail to the northeast.

5 Grey-Bruce Area

Allan Park Conservation Area
LOCATION: From Hanover go east on Hwy. 4 for about 6.5 km, then south on Sideroad 40-41 for about 2.5 km, then west on Conc. 11 to park.
LENGTH: 2.5 km.

This 28 ha park has one trail plus areas for skiers to explore the hardwood bush and till ridges. From these ridges you can look out over the surrounding area and spot the nearby Telesat receiving station. The single trail begins at the south end of a trout pond. For map contact the Saugeen Valley Conservation Authority, RR 1, Hanover, Ont. N4N 3B8.

El Ron Inn Resort
LOCATION: From Flesherton 1.6 km north on Hwy. 10.
LENGTH: 10 km.

Near scenic Beaver Valley area, Suitable for all levels of skiers. Night skiing. Dining room. Accommodation at the resort.

Happy Valley Ski Resort
LOCATION: Off Hwy. 4 about 16 km west of Walkerton.

Several local trails in connection with a downhill resort. Trails pass through woods and open fields in a farming area. Chalet, snack bar, rentals, downhill skiing, lodging in Walkerton. Contact resort at Box 306, Walkerton, Ont. N0G 2V0.

Headquarters Conservation Area
LOCATION: From Hanover south on Bruce County Rd. 10 for 5 km then east on Conc. 17 for 800 m.
LENGTH: 5 km of interlocking trails.

This 60 ha park has trails which can be run in 15 minutes and others which take up to one hour. Hardwood and softwood trees, northern bog, sulphur spring and pond with stream network. This is a year-round wildlife sanctuary. Map and further information from Saugeen Valley Conservation Authority, RR 1, Hanover, Ont. N4N 3B8.

The Homestead Resort
LOCATION: From Durham south 8 km on Hwy. 6, then west 4.8 km on Wilder Lake Rd.
LENGTH: 10 km.

The Homestead is in the heart of the beautiful Saugeen Highlands. The property consists of 300 ha of rolling terrain, approximately 100 ha cleared for a golf course, with the balance in its natural state – bush, streams and a 39 ha lake. Cottages, lodge, restaurant, snack bar. Groomed trails for all levels of ability. Rentals, ski instruction, tour guide, tobogganing and night skiing. 2-way radio patrol on trails. Bus transportation to and from the resort. Accommodation at resort or contact Grey-Bruce Tourist Council, RR 4, Owen Sound, Ont.

Minto Glen Ski Club
LOCATION: From east side of Harrison north on Hwy. 89, then follow County Rd. 2. Total of 10 km from town.
LENGTH: 10 km of loop trails.

Minto Glen was originally a downhill resort but added groomed cross-country trails on its 39 ha property. Hilly farm and mixed woods. Rentals, snack bar, cookout shelter. Resort open weekends and holidays. Map available.

Mount Forest Conservation Area (Angus Smith)
LOCATION: 1 km south of Mount Forest on Hwy. 6, then west on Arthur Sideroad.

Cross-country skiing on about 4 ha, near Saugeen R.

Pike Lake Lodge
LOCATION: From Mount Forest 6.5 km west on Hwy. 89.

Mixed farm and wood area near Saugeen R. Night skiing, skating, snack bar. Accommodation at the lodge.

Saugeen Bluffs
LOCATION: From Paisley north on County Rd. 3 about 5 km, then west on marked access road.

This 140 ha conservation area overlooks the Saugeen R. Area is generally mixed agricultural with farm and pasture land, but along the river there are many treed spots remaining. Skiers have a choice of relatively flat table lands atop the banks or the sometimes steep slopes of the riverbank. More level areas are found along the shore of the river itself. Ice should be tested before use.

Saugeen Highlands
LOCATION: Centred around Saugeen R., crossing Hwy. 4 between Flesherton and Durham.
LENGTH: About 200 km.

The trail system has been created by a group of resorts in the Durham area. They wander over rolling agricultural land cleared for crops and pasture, and through woodlot sections. At several points they cross the frozen Saugeen R. or wander along the cut it has made in the soft soil.

Stonehills Sun 'N' Snow Park
LOCATION: From Durham, east 11 km on Hwy. 4, then south 4.8 km on County Rd. 23 (Dromore Rd.)
LENGTH: 10 km.

Situated in the Saugeen Highlands. Varied terrain: rolling hills, woods and some open spaces. Suitable for all levels of ability. Skating, tobogganing and night skiing. Accommodation on premises or write Grey-Bruce Tourist Council, RR 4, Owen Sound, Ont.

MacGregor Point Provincial Park
LOCATION: On L. Huron shoreline south of Port Elgin.

This 400 ha park has ski and hiking trails which start near park office and wind through a mixture of maple forest and meadow land to the south. Land tends to be bumpy in some areas and flat in others.

6 Kitchener-Waterloo Area

Aberfoyle Country Club
LOCATION: Just south of Guelph. From Aberfoyle go east on Wellington Rd. for 3 km.
LENGTH: 31 km.

There is cross-country and downhill skiing at this resort. Three cross-country trails for beginner to advanced skiers range from 6 to 15 km through open woodlands with rolling hills. Night-time cross-country skiing. Resort closed Mondays. Rentals, instruction, racing program and food. For more information write Aberfoyle Country Club, RR 1, Puslinch, Ont. or phone (519) 822-5764 or 821-1050.

Chicopee
LOCATION: South of Kitchener with access off Hwy. 8 via Freeport and Morrison Roads.
LENGTH: About 4 km.

Skiing on more than 40 ha including conservation area lands and near Chicopee, the downhill resort first established in the hilly countryside. Grooming, rentals, lessons, snack bar.

Conestogo Conservation Area
LOCATION: North of Waterloo. Conestogo Dam at Conestogo L. 800 km southwest of Drayton.
LENGTH: Loop trail of 35 km.

The trail passes through hardwood bushes, plantations, agricultural and recreational lands. Trail groomed and marked. Accommodation in the Kitchener-Waterloo area or in Listowel.

Elora Gorge
LOCATION: North of Guelph. From Elora south on Elora Rd. 2 km.

The Elora Gorge, located in a 100 ha conservation area, is one of the major natural land features in Southern Ontario. The Grand R. passes between steep rock walls and provides exceptional scenery. Most skiing is on about 8 km of hiking trails.

Pinehurst Conservation Area
LOCATION: On east side of Hwy. 94A, 6.5 km north of Paris.

There are no marked ski trails. Skiers use a series of nature trails along the forested slopes and ski on the unplowed park roads. This 103 ha park is centred around a 9 ha spring-filled kettle lake, one of many in the Dumfries area. Around the lake the land is gently rolling upland hardwood with more than 100 species of trees and shrubs. Picnic shelter and barbecues.

7 Niagara Peninsula

Bronte Creek Provincial Park
LOCATION: Burlington area, west of Hwy. 25 (Bronte Rd.) From Queen Elizabeth Way just west of Hwy. 25 take North Service Rd. in westerly direction then turn north on Burloak Dr. to park entrance.
LENGTH: 11 km of loops.

System of trails is mainly over pasture and wooded areas. Park staff recommends avoiding Bronte Creek Ravine because of 30 m dropoff. Trails are marked and groomed. Picnic pavilions with electricity, washrooms, picnic tables and barbecues at parking lots, skating and tobogganing, sleigh rides. Children's barn and Spruce Lane Farm, a turn-of-the-century farm, open for visits. Park fees. Maps and brochures at area. For more information write Bronte Creek Provincial Park, 1470 Bronte Road North, RR 2, Oakville, Ont. L6J 4Z3.

Cedar Springs Ski Club, Burlington
LOCATION: Burlington. From Hwy. 5 north on Cedar Springs Rd. to club.
LENGTH: 2 km.

Small, groomed trail around a downhill ski area, which is mainly open weekends. Snack bar, instruction, fee.

Valens Conservation Area
LOCATION: North from Hamilton on Hwy. 6 to Freelton, then west on Hwy. 97 about 5 km to entrance on north side.
LENGTH: 6 km of trails on 280 ha of land.

This is a rolling, partly wooded area with two trails. Wildlife includes deer, fox, raccoon and small animals. Trails marked with orange tape. Parking lot, warm-up hut with waxing area. Skating on large reservoir. Map from Hamilton Region Conservation Authority, Box 99, 838 Mineral Springs Rd., Ancaster, Ont. L9G 3L3.

Chedoke Winter Sports Park
LOCATION: Hamilton on Aberdeen Ave. near Hwy. 403.

Cross-country skiing on 30 ha of land around a small, downhill ski resort. Snack bar.

Hamilton Cross-Country Ski Club
LOCATION: South of Hamilton. From Binbrook on Hwy. 56, take Golf Club Rd.

A 32 km creek runs throughout the 160 ha property. Gently rolling, wooded terrain with open spaces. Some wildlife may be observed. Open weekends, instruction may be arranged, rentals, pro shop, waxing area, food and liquor. Some grooming. Accommodation in Hamilton.

Dundas Valley Trails
LOCATION: Ancaster off Mineral Springs Rd. and Ancaster Rd.
LENGTH: About 10 km. Can form a loop of about 3 hr.

Dundas Valley trails are on three tracts of conservation authority land at Ancaster. Area is wooded and hilly, considered intermediate terrain. Trails groomed. Map available from Hamilton Region Conservation Authority, Box 99, 838 Mineral Springs Rd., Ancaster, Ont. L9G 3L3.

Christie Conservation Area
LOCATION: West from Hamilton 32 km on Hwy. 5.
LENGTH: Main loop of 5.5 km with three small cutoffs. Time about 2 hr.

This is a 336 ha area with hilly, wooded and open areas. Trails marked and groomed. Warm-up area, food, skating, tobogganing, fire pit. Map at trail or from Hamilton Region Conservation Authority, Box 99, 838 Mineral Springs Rd., Ancaster, Ont. L9G 3L3.

Chippawa Creek Conservation Area
LOCATION: West of Welland. From Wellandport Village follow Regional Rd. 45 (Creek Rd.) west 2.5 km on south side of Welland.
LENGTH: 5.9 km of loop trails.

Three small trail systems are located in this 146 ha park along the south side of the river. Two short nature trails are in south part of the area and a route following roads and pathways is in the north section. All trails begin at the parking lot by the gatehouse. Terrain of open fields, bush and hedgerows. Brochures and maps available from the Niagara Peninsula Conservation Authority, Box 460, Fonthill, Ont. L0S 1E0.

Fonthill Ski Centre
LOCATION: Near Welland. From Hwy. 20 in Fonthill north 8 km on Lookout Point Rd.
LENGTH: 3 km on 64 ha.

Located on golf course, groomed, rentals on weekend. Lodging in town and Niagara Falls region.

Pine Valley Golf Club
LOCATION: From Simcoe west 11 km on Hwy. 24 to golf club.
LENGTH: A network of trails ranging from about 1 km to 10 km.

Wooded and rolling countryside beside Turkey Point Provincial Park. Trails pass through Spooky Hollow Nature Sanctuary. Washrooms and rest area at Normandale Provincial Fish Hatchery along Red Trail. Map at starting point. Trail maintained by Norfolk Cross-Country Skiers and Hikers. Rentals, instruction and ski clinics. Accommodation information from Simcoe Chamber of Commerce, Simcoe, Ont.

8 Greater Toronto Area

Many skiers in the massive urban area of Toronto first tested their new equipment and learned to kick and glide on parts of the 4000 ha of parkland. There is a wide variety of terrain, ranging from flat fields to very scenic ravines and river valleys. While some parks are suitable only for a quick dash through a fresh fall of snow, others are extensive enough to permit an afternoon's excursion.

A few have trails marked for skiers and offer such services as waxing huts, lessons, barbecues and even chalets. Most have walking or bicycle trails which can be used for skiing.

Some skiers set their own tracks in little used areas and return for daily exercise or race training sessions. After storms, a number of skiers are even seen gliding their merry way along unplowed sidewalks while pedestrians slip and slide at each painful step.

Toronto is not known for its heavy snow cover during most of the winter, but some of the parks are so well groomed one can ski on a dusting of snow. The only problem arises when an area has heavy pedestrian traffic and the snow becomes packed and rough. The best skiing is just after a snowfall or on routes seldom used for walking.

As the jurisdiction over parkland is fragmented between such bodies as the Metro government, six area municipalities, the Metro Zoo and the Metro Toronto and Region Conservation Authority, it sometimes takes research to locate parks and find out how each is developed. One way is to get a road map which has parkland marked clearly in a color such as green, then start visiting. Another way is to phone parks authorities at the following numbers: Metro-367-8186; City of Toronto-367-7251; East York-461-9451; Etobicoke-626-4557; North York-225-4611; Scarborough-438-7411; York-653-2700; Conservation authority-661-6600.

Humber Region

LOCATION: Western section of Metro from northern boundary at Steeles Ave. to L. Ontario along Humber R.
LENGTH: More than 20 km.

The Humber R. forms a spine for the major series of parks in the western part of the city. In a chain that is broken in places, the system starts with the 93 ha Rowntree Mills Park in the north, then the system wends its way south through Summerlea and The Elms. South of Hwy. 401 it picks up with Cruickshank and Raymore, then broadens out in a 60 ha region known as Eglinton Flats. Scarlett Mills, Smythe and Lambton Woods, then a small gap for the Canadian Pacific rail line.

To the south again, in Magwood Park, there are lessons and trails reaching south along the river. Below Bloor St., the river widens and deepens and trails wander through heavy bush. Further south still is an area known as the Humber Marshes. It is full of wildlife, but the swampy nature of much of the land makes skiing an exercise in bushwhacking. For easier skiing in the region there is the 136 ha High Park, with rolling, wooded hills beside Grenadier Pond, to the west. Centennial Park, with 4 of its 80 ha reserved for cross-country skiing, is to the south of Eglinton Ave., west of Hwy. 427.

North York Ski Centre

LOCATION: Earl Bales Park, east side of Bathurst St., south of Sheppard Ave.

The Borough of North York has developed a public ski centre for cross-country and downhill skiers in a park on the former York Downs Golf Course. The 64 ha are a mixture of fields and woods with a large ravine along the west branch of the Don R. This provides a modest hill for the downhill runs and for cross-country skiers on an afternoon outing. The centre has a full ski program including pre-season exercises, ski school, pro shop, rentals, club house and snack bar. For information phone 638-5315.

Finch East Park

LOCATION: North York. Straddles Finch Ave. E. between Bayview Ave. and Leslie St.

This parkland along the east branch of the Don R. is quite hilly and rugged with thick stands of trees and considerable wildlife. Skiing is of the bushwhacking type and travellers pick their own routes over fields and through the trees.

Don Valley Parks

LOCATION: From York Mills Rd. and Bayview Ave. in north, south and east to Victoria Park Ave. north of Danforth Ave.
LENGTH: Chain of parks stretches almost uninterrupted for more than 10 km.

In the north you can start at Windfields Park and ski behind some of the most exclusive estates in Metro. There is a short stretch of private land before the parkland picks up again with Edward's Garden at Lawrence Ave. Here there is a series of paths both beside Wilket Cr. and along the well-treed high ground to the west. The parkland then branches out into Wilket Creek, Sunnybrook and Serena Gundy parks. It also reaches northwest along the west branch of the Don R. to Glendon College campus.

South from this cluster of parks the greenbelt continues under Eglinton Ave. and past the Ontario Science Centre at Ernest Thompson Seton Park. There is a break at the Don Valley Parkway, then Taylor Creek Park stretches along a valley as far as Victoria Park Ave. There is another break for a golf course, then parkland picks up with Byng Park.

Scarborough Parks

LOCATION: Especially along the Highland Creek.
LENGTH: A chain of parks runs along the creek for about 10 km.

Scarborough is the Metro municipality with the most undeveloped land and in the northern regions, particularly around the Metro Zoo, there are many acres of open fields. In the more populated section there are a number of parks along a creek providing scenic trips. Thomson Memorial Park, which runs southeast from Ellesmere Ave. to near McCowan Rd., south of the Civic Centre, has several small trails. Bendale, Hague, McCowan Road, Knob Hill and Cedar Brook form a chain of parks as far as Scarboro Golf and Country Club. Then the large Morningside Park fans out around the creek. Highland Cr. continues through Scarborough College campus and into Colonel Danforth Park on the east side before emptying into L. Ontario.

Metro Toronto Zoo

LOCATION: Northeast corner of Metro Toronto. From Exit 61A on Hwy. 401 north 1.6 km.
LENGTH: 3 and 5 km trails.

The Metro Zoo is one of the finest in the world. It has thousands of animals and plants on 284 ha site in Scarborough. The 3 km Eurasian trail starts near zoo entrance and passes Eurasian and Polar regions before ending at restaurant. Passes Bactrian (two-humped) camels, Siberian tigers, Chinese leopards, dromedaries, yaks, Barbary apes and Polar bears. African trail of 5 km skirts rim of Rouge R. valley giving good view of Canadian Animal Domain. Free maps at ticket booth, regular zoo admission, open seven days a week all year. Call 284-0123 for snow report. Hours: 10 A.M. to 4:30 P.M. Last admission, 3:30.

Claireville Conservation Area

LOCATION: Northwest edge of Metro Toronto. Main access south off Hwy. 7 west of Hwy. 50.

Claireville has 600 ha of land, mostly open fields, with some wooded areas. The west branch of the Humber R. traverses the parkland and has been dammed at one point to create a large reservoir. The country is rolling and in many places exposed to wind, so skiers should choose their areas according to weather.

Albion Hills Conservation Area

LOCATION: From Bolton 8 km north on Hwy. 50.
LENGTH: Loop trails of 1.7, 2.6, 2.7, 5.8, 7.6 km. Graded beginner to intermediate.

Undulating terrain typical of the Oak Ridges moraine area, both open and wooded areas in natural and reforestation plots. Trail grooming. Refreshment booth and chalet-type shelter available on weekends only. Skating, downhill skiing, tobogganing and snowshoeing areas adjacent to the ski trails. Rental service available and interpretive hikes scheduled on weekends. Motel accommodation at Bolton, but area within a 64 km drive from Metropolitan Toronto. Free maps available at area. Holds regular ski events. Fees.

Palgrave Forest and Wildlife Area

LOCATION: Just west of Palgrave. From Hwy. 50 just south of Palgrave go west 3 km on Sideroad 25 then north on unpaved road for about the same distance to trail access points along road or off parking lot.
LENGTH: 16 km of loop trails.

This Metropolitan Toronto and Region Conservation Authority forest has a mixture of pine plantations and mixed bush with some open, swamp areas. It is very hilly and criss-crossed with a number of streams. Though there are trails rated from novice through intermediate, many of them require intermediate or better ability in order to climb and especially to descend some of the steep slopes with safety. Trails groomed and open weekends and holidays. Trail fee. Maps at area.

Terra Cotta Conservation Area
LOCATION: 1.6 km north of Village of Terra Cotta on Conc. 11, Halton Hills Twp.
LENGTH: 5 km.

Conservation area of 124 ha is open daily. Trails wind through wooded areas and meadows with some hilly areas. Partly on Bruce Trail. Skirts highly scenic river valley. Area for cookouts and small lake with skating. Operated by Credit Valley Conservation Authority. Trails are not groomed.

Boyd Conservation Area
LOCATION: Just north of Toronto. From Woodbridge on Hwy. 7 go north 3 km on Islington Ave. to parking lot.

This 400 ha park in a valley of the Humber R. has rolling terrain used for cross-country skiing and tobogganing. Skiers pack their own trails along the valley and many follow the winding course of the river south as far as Woodbridge. Parking fee.

Summit Golf Course
LOCATION: Richmond Hill. In north end of town on east side of Hwy. 11 just south of Gormley Sideroad.
LENGTH: 25 km of interconnecting loops.

The Summit Golf and Country Club is one of the original ski areas in the Metro Toronto region. Trails wind over the fairways and through a mixture of hard and softwood forests. There are hills and flat terrain. Rated for all abilities. Ski area is run by Richmond Hill Parks and Recreation Dept. Instructions, rentals, snack bar, shelter, maps, ski patrol on weekends. For more information contact Richmond Hill Parks and Recreation Dept. (416) 884-8101, ext. 74 or 75.

Seneca College Ski Trails
LOCATION: North of Toronto. From Hwy. 400 east 5 km on King City Sideroad, through King City, then north 3 km on Dufferin St. to college entrance.
LENGTH: 11 km plus skiing on 16 ha lake.

The King Campus of Seneca College is located on 280 ha of wooded parkland. Skiing through rolling woodland, some swamp and over frozen surface of lake. Skiers use sloping front lawn of the former Eaton mansion for learning downhill techniques. This campus specializes in recreation and outdoor education courses, including a number related to cross-country skiing. Rentals, instruction, snack bar, waxing area and ski shop. Trail fee. Lessons days and evenings, ski touring and leadership. Trips to Haliburton for weekend skiing and winter camping trips. Winter survival and wilderness first aid. Pre-season and racing courses.

Mill Run-Toronto Ski Club
LOCATION: From Uxbridge west 9.5 km on Aurora Sideroad.
LENGTH: Varied trails on 240 ha.

Mill Run Golf Club is used as a weekend cross-country area by the Toronto Ski Club. Terrain is picturesque and ranges from open fairways to woods with flat and rolling sections. Club house, snack bar, barbecues, ski instruction by appointment, trail fees. Information from ski club at 8 Colborne St., Toronto, N1S E1E

Bruce's Mill Conservation Area
LOCATION: Between Woodbine Ave. and Hwy. 48 on the Gormley-Stouffville Sideroad.
LENGTH: 8 km of loops.

Novice and intermediate trails on Metro Toronto and Region Conservation Authority area. Rolling to flat terrain with trails through sugar bush, spruce bog and some reforested areas. Open daily, instruction, trails groomed, rentals, refreshments, washrooms, warm-up area, skating, tobogganing, maple syrup demonstration from mid-March to mid-April. Parking fee. Map at area.

Claremont Conservation Area
LOCATION: Northeast of Metro Toronto. From Brougham, east 3 km on Hwy. 7.
LENGTH: 16 km of loop trails.

Three trail systems for different levels of skiers loop through rolling terrain. Open areas and forests of mixed hardwood bush and reforested areas. Novice trail of 1.6 km, intermediate of 5.6 km and advanced trail of 8.6 km. This Metro Toronto and Region Conservation Authority area is open weekends and holidays. Nature interpretation program planned for trails. Trail fee. Maps at area.

Ski Woodnewton
LOCATION: From Claremont follow Brock Rd. north 8 km to Coppins Corners, turn east on Durham Rd. 21 1.6 km, go north of 6th Con. of Uxbridge Twp. 1.6 km.

LENGTH: 10 km of interlocking trails in 3 loops.

Scenic wooded trails utilizing a ridge of hills 46 m high. Trails graded easy, intermediate and expert. Rentals, snack bar, trail grooming, cookout. Open daylight hours daily, except Monday and Tuesday. Accommodation available at Whitby, Oshawa, Toronto. Maps posted on trails, sheet maps available.

Cold Creek Conservation Area

LOCATION: Between Bolton and Nobleton. From King Sideroad go north 3 km on Concession 11.
LENGTH: 13 km of loop trails.

There are trails of 1.5, 4.5 and 7 km, for different skiing abilities, over gently rolling terrain. Primarily open area with some bush and spruce bog. Trails open daily, groomed, maps at area, heated shelter, refreshment booth on weekends, parking fee. Area also has tobogganing, husky dog races and game dog trials on weekends. Maintained by Metro Toronto and Region Conservation Authority.

North Pickering Hiking Trail

LOCATION: Along Duffin Creek at eastern edge of Metro Toronto. Access points on Hwy 7, just east of Green River Village, Whitevale Village on Concession 5 and Camp Picada, off Conc. 3, just west of Brock Rd.
LENGTH: 13 km hiking and walking trail, much of which is suitable for skiing, depending on snow conditions.

The trail and its surrounding woodlands, bordered by farms, is a conservation project of the North Pickering Development Corp., which is creating a town in the area. More than 400 ha of relatively wild land have been preserved along the West Duffin Valley. The northern section of the trail, described as the Heritage Trail, is relatively flat and skiable. Running between the villages of Whitevale and Green River, it passes an old grist mill. South of Whitevale the trail enters the "wilderness" section and the further south one goes the steeper the river bank becomes. Most of this area is more suitable for expert skiers and at times the banks become too hard-packed for most skis. The southern link is again on relatively easy terrain with flat stretches and some large hills to the east side, suitable for practising telemark turns when the snow is deep and soft. A detailed trail map is available from the North Pickering Development Corp., Ontario Ministry of Housing, 950 Yonge St., Toronto Ont. M7A 2M1 or telephone (416) 965-9168.

Sibbald Point Provincial Park

LOCATION: South shore of L. Simcoe, 4.8 km east of Sutton, 1.6 km north of Hwy. 48.
LENGTH: 9.6 km loop.

Level terrain, partially wooded and open. Trails are marked and groomed and used for both snowshoeing and cross-country skiing. Trail map. Skating rink, snowmobile trail. Open 7 days a week, entry fee. Camping in the park, electrical outlets, firewood. Cross-country ski races in conjunction with the Sutton Winter Carnival, organized by Chamber of Commerce, Sutton. Motels on Highway 48 and in Jackson's Point. For brochure and information, write the Park Superintendent, RR 2, Sutton West, Ont.

9 Oshawa Area

Dagmar Ski Resort

LOCATION: North of Oshawa. On road between Claremont and Ashburn.
LENGTH: 20 km of loop trails.

This resort has both cross-country and downhill skiing. There are two cross-country trails, a 5-km beginner run through mainly open country with gentle hills and a 15-km advanced trail in wooded terrain with some steep sections. There are lights on 2 km of the trails. From the height of land here one can see L. Ontario and high points such as the CN Tower in downtown Toronto. Downhill area has 60 m vertical rise. Open daily, instruction, rentals, groomed trails, cafeteria, family-type race, maps available. For more information write Dagmar Resort Ltd., RR 1, Ashburn, Ont. L0B 1A0.

Durham County Forest

LOCATION: North 16 km from Newcastle on Hwy. 115.
LENGTH: About 20 km.

Two marked hiking trails, red and blue, start from car park but there are other forest roads which can be used to add several more kilometres to any trip. Suitable for all levels of ability. Main trails lead past Lookout Hill which gives view of downhill Kirby Ski Area to south. No patrols, so skiers should be equipped with map, compass and some emergency supplies. It should be noted this is a popular area with snowmobilers. Topographic map of 1:50,000 scale is Scugog sheet. Primitive toilets at car park. Restaurants in Kirby area just to south.

Enniskillen Conservation Area
LOCATION: Bowmanville area. North of Hampton Village. From Durham Regional Rd. 57 (Scugog Rd.) go west on 7th Conc. 2 km then north on Road 10 1 km.
LENGTH: 4.5 km series of loops.

This series of trails criss-crosses the Bowmanville Creek on bridges in a generally flat area. Some marked trails, maps at area, heated shelter, food and sleigh rides on weekends, skating on pond, tobogganing, snowshoeing. The park is on 35 ha of rolling fields, woodlands, ponds and creek bottomlands. The area is a historic site. The Boyne Water Mills were established here in 1847 with a grist mill, which is long gone and an earthen dam, which is still present. For map and information contact Central Lake Ontario Conservation Authority, 1650 Dundas St. E., Whitby, Ont. L1N 2K8 or phone (416) 579-0411.

Heber Down Conservation Area
LOCATION: North of Whitby. From Hwy. 401 go north 3 km on Brock St., west 1 km on Taunton Rd., then north 1 km on Country Lane.
LENGTH: 6.5 km series of loops.

This series of trails crosses level country with mixture of woods and open areas, including Hydro and pipeline corridors. One trail passes an old sawmill then swings east and north toward the Eastlynde Creek. For map and information contact the Central Lake Ontario Conservation Authority, 1650 Dundas St. E., Whitby, Ont. L1N 2K8 or phone (416) 579-0411.

Kendal Recreation Area
LOCATION: North of Newcastle on County Rd. 9 between Kirby and Kendal.

The area has a snowmobile trail and a separate area for cross-country skiers, snowshoers and tobogganers. Parking, skating rink, washrooms.

Mosport Park Ltd.
LOCATION: From Bowmanville north 19 km on Liberty St.

For much of the year this internationally known race track does not hear the whine of super-tuned engines and the scream of tires. It is actually situated on 280 ha of peaceful farming country suitable for such activities as cross-country skiing. Instruction, rentals, snack bar, trail fee. Open weekends.

10 Orangeville – Bradford Area

Luther Marsh
LOCATION: West of Orangeville. Marked access points from Hwys. 9 and 89.
LENGTH: 35 km.

The Luther Marsh Wildlife Management Area is one of the major wildlife and waterfowl refuges in Southern Ontario. The trail wanders through a variety of uplands and wetlands, forest plantations and agricultural land. It passes nearby the Egerton Esker, a leatherleaf bog and Luther L. A rich variety of birds and mammals may be observed in this area. Trail is groomed and marked. Accommodation in Arthur, Orangeville, Fergus and Mount Forest, all about 25 to 32 km from Luther.

Hockley Hills Resort
LOCATION: From Orangeville north of Hwys. 10 and 24, then east on Hockley Rd. for a total of 6.4 km.
LENGTH: Small trails for instruction, skiing on Bruce Trail.

Situated in Hockley Valley, with flat sections and gently rolling hills. Instruction, rentals, pro shop, snowmobiling. Closed Mondays. Hotel with swimming pool, sauna, dining room, cafeteria, lounge with nightly entertainment and dancing. Basically a downhill resort. Maps available.

Hockley Valley Winter Park
LOCATION: From Orangeville north on Hwy. 10, then east about 10 km on Hockley Valley Rd.
LENGTH: 9 km.

Another of the six resorts in this part of the Nottawasaga Valley, Hockley Valley is located on 46 metre high slopes. The valley is a highly scenic area with broad bottom lands and complicated contours on the hillsides. Downhill resort open weekends with snack bar.

Cedar Springs Ski Club, Orangeville
LOCATION: North from Orangeville on Hwy. 10, then east 10 km on Hockley Valley Rd.
LENGTH: 2 km.

This is one of six small ski resorts located in the Hockley Valley of the Nottawasaga R. Both cross-country and downhill skiing at this development. Great variety of terrain. Several streams and the river have created a highly varied valley pattern.

Valley Schuss Ski Club
LOCATION: From Hwy. 10 north of Orangeville go east 13 km on Hockley Valley Rd. From Airport Rd. west 1.5 km.
LENGTH: About 3 km.

Trail heads out from the Valley Schuss downhill ski resort in the Hockley Valley. It crosses the Bruce Trail.

Scanlon Creek Conservation Area
LOCATION: From Bradford north 4 km on Hwy. 11.
LENGTH: Loop trail of 4.8 km.

Trail is on combination of open and wooded, flat and rolling terrain in L. Simcoe area. Located at Prof. E. A. Smith Natural Resources Educational Centre. For information contact South Lake Simcoe Conservation Authority, Box 282, Newmarket, Ont. L3Y 4X1.

The Briars Resort
LOCATION: On the south shore of L. Simcoe near Jackson's Point. From village of Sutton go north on Dalton Rd. or York Rd. 18 to Hedge Rd.
LENGTH: About 10 km of trails on property plus skiing on golf course and on lake when ice is safe.

The Briars Resort and Conference Centre is a resort hotel on 80 ha of level countryside treed with pines and maples and cut by small streams. There are trails marked on the property plus skiing in the surrounding area. Hotel has day and night skating. Baby sitting arranged.

Ponderosa Campground Ski Resort
LOCATION: Mount Albert, south of L. Simcoe.
LENGTH: 12 km on five trails.

The campground, off Hwy. 48, has three intermediate trails of about 3 km each and two short beginner trails in wooded area. Wildlife includes grouse and rabbits. Routes are used as nature trails in summer. Groomed and marked trails. Rentals, instruction, snack bar, winter camping, trail maps. For information write Ponderosa Campground, Box 53, Mount Albert, Ont.

11 Nottawasaga Bay

Kolapore Uplands Ski Trails
LOCATION: Beaver Valley Region. From Thornbury south about 19.5 km on County Rd. 2 to junction with County Rd. 19. From there south about 1.6 km to start on west side of road just south of bridge.
LENGTH: Series of trails totalling 35 km.

This network was developed in 1973 by the University of Toronto Outing Club. Trails run mainly through hilly, forested country. Some suitable for beginners but most for experienced skiers. Marked with triangular orange blazes. Club notes much land is privately owned and to preserve good relations with persons who allow its use, skiers are asked to stay on trails, carry out garbage and not build fires. Trails are marked with such colorful names as Wandering Rocks, Quiet Pastures, Labyrinth, Red Death Hill and Wild Mouse. Detailed map available from club: Kolapore Uplands Ski Trail, c/o University of Toronto Outing Club, Box 6647, Stn. A, Toronto, Ont. M5W 1X4.

Talisman Ski Resort
LOCATION: In Beaver Valley. From Flesherton on Hwy. 10 east on Hwy 4 for 3.2 km, north on County Rd. 13 through Eugenia and Kimberley. Resort 1.6 km northeast of Kimberley.
LENGTH: 10 km.

Talisman Ski Resort was developed in mid-1960s as a major ski and year-round resort. Cross country trails lead from resort through scenic Beaver Valley area. Excellent views from top of Niagara Escarpment on either side of valley. Valley bottom is mixed farmland and woods with Beaver R. passing through area. Restaurants, bar, rentals, ski shop, lessons from Lorne McFadgen Ski School. Tobogganing and extensive downhill skiing. Winter carnival. Lodge accommodation plus hotels and farmhouses in area. Talisman Ski Resort, Kimberley, Ont.

Bud's Place
LOCATION: Kimberley, in the Beaver Valley.
LENGTH: 23 km of loops.

This cross-country resort lies on the west side of the Beaver R. between Beaver Valley and Talisman ski areas. Trails form a series of loops through open areas and pine and hardwood bush, in the scenic Beaver Valley. Trails groomed, rentals, instruction, food, shelters and ski shop with repair area. Extensive accommodation in Kimberley area. For more information contact: Bud's Place, Kimberley, Ont. N0C 1G0 or phone (519) 599-5096.

Georgian Peaks Ski Resort
LOCATION: From Thornbury Hwy. 26 east 6.5 km.
LENGTH: 14 km of loop trails.

Georgian Peaks, which has the highest downhill runs in Central Canada, also has cross-country trails running from the area along the Niagara Escarpment. The terrain is wooded and at places almost mountainous but suitable for all levels. Scenery is very good with excellent views of Georgian Bay, which is very close to resort. Instruction, rentals, restaurant, groomed trails, shelter, bar and dancing. Downhill races. Accommodation nearby and information from Grey-Bruce Regional Council, RR 4, Owen Sound.

Cyril's Cross-Country Ski Centre
LOCATION: From Collingwood west 9.6 km on Hwy. 26, then south 1.6 km on Arrowhead Rd.
LENGTH: 2 trails, 3 and 5 km. Travel time 1 to 2 hr.

Located on wooded, mountainous terrain of the Niagara Escarpment. First level suited for beginners, top for advanced skiers. Spectacular view. Rentals, snack bar, instruction, shelter, downhill facilities nearby. For accommodation, contact Grey-Bruce Regional Tourist Council, RR 4 Owen Sound, Ont. or Blue Mountain Lodging Assn., RR 3, Collingwood, Ont.

Tyrolean Village Resort
LOCATION: From Collingwood follow Hwy. 26 8 km west, then south 1.6 km to resort entrance.
LENGTH: 10 km of trails.

Tyrolean Village is a development at the foot of the Niagara Escarpment and beside the Blue Mountain Ski Resort, which has downhill and cross-country facilities. The cross-country trails at Tyrolean are in hilly, wooded and open country and provide good views of Georgian Bay. They are suitable for all levels of skiers. Accommodation, food and such facilities as indoor tennis available at resort. Rentals and lessons nearby.

Blue Mountain Ski Resort
LOCATION: From Collingwood take Hwy. 26 8 km west, then south 1.6 km on Blue Mountain Winter Park Rd. to the ski resort.
LENGTH: 34 km of trails with travel time up to 5 hr.

Blue Mountain is one of the largest downhill ski resorts in Central Canada and in recent years has started a cross-country development. The downhill runs are spread across 4 km of the Niagara Escarpment facing Georgian Bay and there is a large development of lodges, ski shops and chalets at the foot of the hills. The cross-country skiing includes groomed trails at the foot and top of the 230-metre-high escarpment with both wooded and open country and the possibility of long downhill runs if the snow conditions are right and the cross-country skier capable of sustained turns. There is even a ski jump for the more daring.

Accommodation, food, bars, dancing, rentals, instructions. Trails groomed. The area features several downhill races including the pro circuit. Accommodation information from Blue Mountain Lodging Assn., RR 3, Collingwood or Grey-Bruce Regional Tourist Council, RR 4, Owen Sound.

Wasaga Beach Provincial Park
LOCATION: From Wasaga Beach east on Hwy. 92 to River Rd. W., then south 400 m.
LENGTH: Loop trails of 4.6, 6.2, 9 km. Travel time from 1 to 3 hr.

The trails are located in a provincially significant natural area. The combination of various sand dune features and rare plant life make this area unique in Ontario. Wildlife includes ruffed grouse, red fox, porcupine, deer and numerous species of birds. Graded novice to advanced. Two shelters with provisions for warming light lunches. Snowshoeing. Nottawasaga Ski Club annual cross-country races second week of February. Accommodation in Wasaga Beach. Contact Chamber of Commerce. Brochures available at beginning of trails.

Nottawasaga Inn
LOCATION: East of Alliston. From Hwy. 400 west about 10 km on Hwy. 89.
LENGTH: 4 km.

Skiing on rolling countryside is free to guests of inn. There is a trail fee for day visitors. Lodging, food, rentals.

Honeywood Ski Centre
LOCATION: From Mansfield north 9.5 km on Airport Rd., then west on Sideroad 25 for

75

9.5 km and south on 1st line West 500 m.

The 488 metre elevation of the farm provides attractive scenery and good snow conditions for the area. The only marked trail is a section of the Bruce Trail which passes through the farm. Otherwise you choose your own routes on 600 ha. Simple dormitory accommodations for 16 in old farmhouse, meals and, by arrangement, instruction. Limited rental equipment. For information contact Honeywood Ski Touring Centre, RR 3, Shelburne, Ont. L0N 1S0.

Mansfield Forest Club
LOCATION: North of Mansfield 4 km on Airport Rd. Downhill resort on west side and cross-country and snowmobile areas just to north on east side of Airport Rd.
LENGTH: 33 km.

This resort has developed attractive land along the Pine R. into a winter sports centre with each activity slightly separated. The cross-country ski trails wander over flat land in the river valley and climb a scenic area known as Oak Ridges. There are good lookouts from several places. Area has full services including food, instruction, rentals and maps for marked and groomed trails. Trail fee.

Minnesing Swamp
LOCATION: West of Barrie about 15 km
LENGTH: A swamp area of several hundred hectares.

This area in Southern Ontario acts as a wildlife refuge and water reservoir. It is shot through with rivers and streams including the Nottawasaga, Pine, Willow and Mad. Bounded on north by Hwy. 26, south by Hwy. 90 and east by little-used Canadian National Railways line, which some skiers use for access. No developed ski trails and snow is often too deep and brush too heavy for snowmobiles. Anyone entering this area should be prepared and equipped for wilderness travel. For map use 1:50,000 Barrie West topographic series. Swamp area is centre of map.

Ski Haven
LOCATION: Take Hwy. 400 north to Hwy. 89. Exit east on Cookstown Rd. 9.5 km toward L. Simcoe.
LENGTH: Loop trails of 16 km on 240 ha.

Trails for all skiers. Beginners use golf course trails. More experienced skiers use wooded and hilly farm land. Trails marked and groomed. Ski shop, rentals, barbecue areas with fireplace, shelter, picnic tables, large, heated area for changing and waxing skis, night skiing parties and bird feeders in clearings. Complete clubhouse facilities, licenced lounge, coffee shop and banquet room. Races. For lodging information contact Ontario Tourist Assn. Hwy. 400, Barrie, Ont. Also accommodation in Nottawasaga Inn, Alliston, and 400 Motel at junction of Hwy. 400 and Hwy. 89. Trail maps available free of charge at clubhouse or write Roy Moe, Ski Haven, Gilford, Ont.

Molson's Park
LOCATION: Just south of Barrie. From Hwy. 400 exit east on Essa Rd., then south on Fairview Service Rd. Park is located on farm just south of brewery.
LENGTH: 16 km.

The cross-country ski centre is operated as a free public relations gesture by Molson's Breweries and includes free instruction. Trails range over 240 ha of farmland and bush. Some trails pass through a tree farm. Trails marked, groomed and graded beginner through advanced. Rentals available but skiers seeking them on weekdays should check with centre to see if equipment is available, as it is sometimes booked by groups. Skating pond, snack bar, tobogganing. Flea market on weekends offers local crafts and antiques.

Horseshoe Valley Resort
LOCATION: Northeast of Barrie. From Hwy. 400 east 8 km on Horseshoe Valley Rd.
LENGTH: 64 km in nine trails on 800 ha.

This is one of the original major cross-country resorts in Ontario. It has been developed since the mid-1960s and is used by skiers from beginner to racing ability. Terrain ranges from flat previously farmed areas now reforested through gently rolling hardwood forests to challenging slopes for expert skiers. Trails groomed and tracks set. Rest stations on long trails. Downhill skiing. Large chalet with licensed lounge, snack bar, rentals, repairs, ski shop, instruction. Babysitting. Maps. Open 9 a.m. to 4:30 p.m. weekdays, 8:30 to 4 p.m. weekends and holidays. Lodging information from Barrie Chamber of Commerce, Fred Grant Sq., Barrie, Ont.; Huronia Tourist Assn., County Building, Midhurst; Orillia Chamber of Commerce, Sundial Dr., Orillia.

Snow Valley Resorts
LOCATION: From Barrie north on Hwy. 27,

then west on Snow Valley Rd. to resort.
LENGTH: About 9 km.

Located on 120 ha of hilly land beside a downhill ski resort in a heavy snow belt area Rentals, instruction, food. Trail fee.

Mountain View Ski Area
LOCATION: 1.6 km west of Midland. Follow ski area signs from Hwy. 27.
LENGTH: Trails of 2.5 and 5 km and many touring areas using part of trails. Loop from clubhouse.

Trails wander through pine and hardwoods and open fields. Terrain is varied with flat lands and gently rolling hills. Open daily, rentals on weekends when no reservation needed, or by reservation during the week. Lunch counter and heated chalet. Trails marked and groomed. Downhill facilities. Accommodation nearby. Trail map posted outside clubhouse. Annual race about first weekend of January. For information contact Don Foster, RR 2, Midland, Ont.

Fern Resort
LOCATION: From Orillia take Hwy. 12 B south to Atherley, then northeast 3.2 km on Rama Rd.
LENGTH: Travel time 1 to 2 hr. and extensive travel possible on L. Couchiching.

Resort estate has nearly 2 km of private lakeshore. Open terrain, wooded, good for beginners. Instruction, rentals. Trails groomed. Entertainment, licensed dining room and lounge, indoor pool, sauna, California hot tub, floodlit skating rink, curling, ping-pong, pool tables, snowmobiling. Resort situated in Huronia ski country. Babysitting can be arranged. Inn and cottage accommodation. For information write Robert and Mary Lou Downing, Fern Resort, RR 5, Orillia, Ont. L3V 6H5.

12 Muskoka

Bracebridge Resource Trails
LOCATION: 6.4 km north of Bracebridge, on the east side of Hwy. 11.
LENGTH: 3 loop trails of 4.8, 6.4, 8 km. Travel time from 30 min. to an hour.

Groomed trails are graded easy to advanced. Wooded area and unplowed bush roads along Muskoka R. The Bracebridge Resource Management Centre is an area of about 600 ha of Crown Land. Known history of the property dates back to 1868-1872, when it was first settled by 12 families under the authority of the "Free Grants and Homesteads Act of 1868."

In 1966 the Crown purchased the "Patterson Property" for the purpose of demonstrating resource management techniques of the Ministry of Natural Resources. Public has an opportunity to view timber, fish, wildlife and recreation. Snowshoeing, hiking. Snowmobiling prohibited. Washroom facilities. Accommodation in Bracebridge. Contact Country Ski and Sports Centre, 72 Manitoba St., Bracebridge, Ont. Maps available at trail and from the Ministry of Natural Resources, Box 1138, Bracebridge, Ont.

Kerr Park
LOCATION: In Bracebridge off Beaumont Dr.
LENGTH: 8 km.

The town and the Muskoka Cross-Country Ski Club operate trails of 2 and 6 km in mixed wooded and open area where intermediate ability is required. Chalet with fireplace and cooking facilities, outdoor barbecue pit and skating pond. Map from Bracebridge Recreation Committee. Site of Bracebridge Langlauf ski tour. More information on this event is available from Gary Adams, Box 2079, Bracebridge, Ont.

Gibson-McCrae Area
LOCATION: From Waubaushene north on Hwy. 69 for 16 km.
LENGTH: 25 km.

Part of a series of wilderness trails cut by the Five Winds Touring Club on Muskoka area Crown Lands, this trail starts at Hwy. 69 and ends at same highway about 3 km north. Trail passes through rugged terrain with mixed hardwoods and softwoods and some open area with a scattering of oak and juniper. It passes below McCrae L., skirts the edge of a Georgian Bay inlet and ends below the Gibson R. There is one ice crossing at McCrae Narrows which must be used with caution. Some steep sections. Club advises most sections call for intermediate ability but skiers should be in good physical condition and led by someone experienced in bushcraft, survival and navigation. Carry food, map, compass, emergency gear. Trails marked with orange or blue tape and paint blazes. Detailed map available from Ministry of Natural Resources office, Parry Sound, or Five Winds Club, 4 Belmont St., Toronto, M5R 1P8.

Coldgray Area
LOCATION: North from Waubaushene on Hwy. 69, 22.5 km to first entry point on west side at Go-Home Lake Rd. Two other entry points off Hwy 69 below Muskoka R.
LENGTH: Loop trails of 8 to 16 km.

Coldgray is the name given a series of connecting trails cut on wilderness Crown Land by the Five Winds Touring Club. They are located between a series of small lakes and streams between the Muskoka R. and Gray L. on the north and Coldwater L. on the south. Terrain is varied with some woods and open fields with juniper and oak. Some areas are rugged and as this is wilderness the club suggests that all parties should be led by someone experienced in survival and navigation. Carry map and compass, spare food and emergency gear. Trails marked with orange or blue plastic tape and paint blazes. Detailed maps available from Ministry of Natural Resources office, Parry Sound, or Five Winds Club, 4 Belmont St., Toronto, M5R 1P8.

Middle Gibson Area
LOCATION: From Port Severn north about 19 km on Hwy. 69, then east 6.5 km on Muskoka Rd. 33 to small parking lot.
LENGTH: More than 50 km.

This is one of a series of wilderness trails cut by the Five Winds Touring Club on Crown Lands in the Muskoka area. The country, long popular with summer visitors, is rugged and scenic with a wide variety of plant and animal life. Trails can be skied by persons of intermediate ability in good physical condition but should be tackled only by groups familiar with wilderness travel and led by experienced skiers with ability in bushcraft, survival and navigation. Carry food, map, compass, spare clothing and emergency gear. Trails marked with orange or blue plastic tape and paint blazes. Detailed maps available from Ministry of Natural Resources office in Parry Sound or from Five Winds Club, 4 Belmont St., Toronto, M5R 1P8.

Muskoka Sands Inn
LOCATION: From Gravenhurst north 5 km on Muskoka Beach Rd.
LENGTH: 10 km.

The inn is beside L. Muskoka in one of the most scenic areas of Ontario and one of the most popular in summer. Skiing through woodlands and on lake.

Tally-Ho Winter Park
LOCATION: From Huntsville east on Hwy. 60 towards Algonquin Park.
LENGTH: 10 km.

This year-round lodge north of the Lake of Bays is located on 20 ha of rolling, forested land. Groomed trails, lodging and food. Rentals and instruction.

Hidden Valley Ski Club
LOCATION: From Huntsville east 8 km on Hwy. 60 and south on access road.
LENGTH: 5 km.

Hidden Valley is one of the largest downhill ski resorts in the Huntsville region and has added cross-country trails on its 20 ha property. Located on shores of Peninsula L. Instruction, rentals, skating, lodging, dining room.

Echo Hills Park
LOCATION: From Huntsville east 16 km on Hwy. 60.
LENGTH: Loop trails of 4.6, 8.5 and 13 km. Travel time 30 to 90 min.

Slightly hilly, mostly heavily wooded area with some open stretches. Some wildlife. Rentals nearby. Trails groomed. Cookout area. Snowshoeing on unplowed road system on 80 ha tract of land. Motels and cottages at Dwight, 2.4 km east of parking area. Map available at entrance. For information write L. R. Cotterchio, Echo Hill Park, RR 2, Huntsville, Ont.

Deerhurst Inn
LOCATION: From Huntsville east on Hwy. 60 then south on Muskoka Road 23.
LENGTH: 25 km.

This lodge on the shore of Peninsula L. was started in 1896 and has developed into a year-round resort. Skiing on winding bush trails, which connect with other local ski trails. Trails groomed and patrolled. Free equipment for guests, lessons, and ski shop. Downhill skiing nearby as part of weekend package. Skating on lake and snowshoeing in bush. Lodge has facilities, including sauna, pool, disco, massage, and evening entertainment. For information write Deerhurst Inn, Box 1950, Huntsville, Ont. P0A 1K0 or phone (705) 789-5543 or use direct Toronto line of 964-3925.

Britannia Hotel Ski Trails
LOCATION: From Huntsville east on Hwy. 35 and 60 for 16 km then south on South Portage Rd. 8 km then left on Britannia Rd.

LENGTH: 4.5 km loop. Travel time 90 min.

Britannia Hotel, RR 2, Huntsville, is a 190-room resort on the Lake of Bays in Muskoka highlands. Area is wooded and hilly with wildlife, beaver dams, lookout. Instruction, rentals, skating, snowshoeing, curling rink, snowmobile rentals, downhill skiing, dining room, bar. Annual loppet.

Cedar Grove Lodge

LOCATION: From Huntsville east 11 km on Hwy. 60.

The lodge has skiing on 40 ha of wooded, hilly terrain. There is food and accommodation.

13 Algonquin

Algonquin Provincial Park

LOCATION: Access to most developed trails from Hwy. 60 starting 44 km east from Huntsville.
LENGTH: More than 100 km.

Algonquin, one of the most evocative words to a canoeist, is now entering the skier's vocabulary as the park slowly starts moving to year-round operations. While the crowds on the portages have become almost oppressive in summer, a winter visitor will find the 7800 sq. km park almost empty of humans. The Ministry of Natural Resources has marked but not groomed five trails off Hwy. 60 and there are limitless possibilities for short or long winter tours through the massive wilderness of the park interior. Starting points of the five trails are given in kilometres from the west gate.

Note: Western Uplands and Highland hiking trails are not designed for skiing and have some steep sections.

Western Uplands Hiking Trail – start from kilometre 3. Three loops of 32, 55 and 71 km wander through the myriad of small lakes in the southwestern part of the park. This is rugged, wooded country for advanced skiers with stamina for a long wilderness trip.

Cache Lake, Old Railway Line – start from kilometre 24. Skiing is possible on the route of an abandoned railway line which once ran across Algonquin Park for about 70 km. The line crosses Hwy. 60 between Tanamakoon and Cache lakes on the south and travels in a generally east-west direction. Skiing suitable for all levels of ability.

Highland Hiking Trail – start from kilometre 32. Two loops of 18 and 35 km. The main trail starts south from Hwy. 60, just west of Pewee L. and the shorter loop circles Provoking L. The longer loop strikes southwest to bluffs just inland from Head L. and skirts the portage trail of 1097 m south to Harness L. It circles back to pick up the small loop south of Provoking L. As in the case of the Western Uplands Trail, skiers should be prepared and equipped for wilderness travel. While this is well-trodden ground in the summer, it is little used in the winter.

Mew Lake to Pog Lake Trail – start at Mew Lake campground or at Pog L., just west of Lake of Two Rivers. Land ranges from flat to gently rolling and is suitable for all abilities. Uses the abandoned railway line for part of its length. 5.5 km trail.

Sunday Lake Trail – start from kilometre 43. A 16 km trail with a loop at end along an old road north from Hwy. 60. The land is quite flat and trail could be used by novice skiers.

In addition to the organized trails, there are many other logging roads which crisscross the park and an immense system of waterways with 80 major canoe routes over 1600 km. There are also a number of other summer access roads around the perimeter of the park which could be skied. A word of caution about trying to adapt canoe routes: parks officials say some ice can be unsafe even in mid-winter and caution should always be used in ice travel. As well, there can be problems in trying to follow portages that are obvious as beaten paths in summer but not evident when snow covered. Some wind up and down very steep slopes. The skier should know the route or check with someone who does.

An increasing number of persons are winter camping here. For starters, the Mew Lake campground at kilometre 32 has a plowed parking lot, firewood and toilets. Campers who head for the interior should be prepared for deep snow and temperatures which can dip as low as minus 40 degrees Celsius. In addition to beautiful views of a frozen wilderness, they will find the tracks of such hardy wildlife as deer, moose, marten, fisher, fox and wolf. The ravens, gray jays and boreal chickadees haunt campsites for stray crumbs. The night silence will be pierced by the cracking of frozen trees and possibly the howling of wolves in the distance.

The western two-thirds of the park is mainly in hardwoods of sugar maple, beech and yellow birch, with hemlock groves and scatterings of giant white pine left over from the major logging era. The drier, sandier eastern section sprouts white, red and jack pine. Spruce bogs occur in low-lying areas throughout the park. The area is sparsely inhabited in winter and there is no gasoline station open for the 70 km between Oxtongue L. on the west and Whitney on the east. Food and lodging in towns. Information from park personnel at east gate (near Whitney) weekdays (8 a.m. to 5 p.m.) and at Park Museum at kilometre 21. Canoe map gives an idea of waterways but is of limited use. Skiers should check with park officials for numbers of topographic maps. Write: District Manager, Algonquin Park District, Box 219, Whitney, Ont. K0J 2M0 or phone (705) 637-2780 or 633-5592.

Algonquin Canoe Routes Ltd.
LOCATION: Whitney, on Hwy. 60 at east gate of Algonquin Provincial Park.
LENGTH: Access to more than 400 km of wilderness trails.

This canoe outfitting and guiding group has a winter operation which uses the vast wilderness in and around Algonquin Park for touring routes. There are trails from 5 km to more than 50 km. The longer routes often require tenting or use of cabins. Terrain varies greatly and includes both flat, lake skiing and high hills. Rentals and guiding available. Accommodation in log base cabin or local motels and lodges. The area is used for tours in early and mid-winter. For more information write Algonquin Canoe Routes Ltd., Box 187, Whitney, Ont. or phone (705) 637-2699.

Bear Trail Inn Resort
LOCATION: At Algonquin Park's east gate, on Hwy. 60, in Whitney, on Galeairy Lake Rd.
LENGTH: Travel time from 1 to 8 hr. Some trails loop, others start 15-20 km inside Algonquin Provincial Park and end at Bear trail.

Most skiing is taking place in Algonquin Provincial Park. In 1975 the first two ski trails were established by the Park's management as part of a larger winter sports program. Ski shop, free guided wilderness tours for groups. Trails marked but not groomed. Snowmobiling, snowshoeing, skating, ice fishing. Licensed dining room. Topographic maps of the area for sale at the resort. For information write Gertrude and Fritz Sorensen, Box 158, Galeairy Lake Rd., Whitney, Ont. K0J 2M0.

Echo Ridge
LOCATION: West of Algonquin Provincial Park. North of Huntsville. 1.6 km east of Kearney, on Hwy. 518.
LENGTH: A wide variety of trails allow trips on old logging roads, traplines and horseback riding trails leading to Algonquin Park.

Groomed trails wander through wilderness bush, past beaver ponds and lakes, over hills with spectacular view over the Almaguin Highlands. Wildlife. Downhill and cross-country skiing instruction available. Pro shop, rentals, survival lessons, packtrips and cookouts arranged. Washrooms, cafeteria, camper parking. Snowshoeing instruction and guide service by reservation. Cross-country races and parties organized. Accommodation in many rustic lodges and cottages. For information, contact Almaguin South Tourist Assn., c/o George Purdy, Lynx Lake, Kearney, Ont. P0A 1M0. Topographic map: Burks Falls S.E. For information on winter carnival, write c/o Kearney Fire Fighters Assn., Kearney, Ont. For more information on resort, write W. Schmidt, Echo Ridge, Box 137, Kearney, Ont. P0A 1M0.

Arrowhead Provincial Park
LOCATION: On the east side of Hwy. 11, 8 km north of Huntsville.
LENGTH: 2 loop trails totalling 14.5 km. Travel time 2½ to 3 hr.

Algonquin type wood and water land, Area and trails ideal for families. Intermediate ability. Washrooms, shelters, winter camping, skating, tobogganing, ice fishing, snowshoeing, snowmobiling. Accommodation in Huntsville. Contact Chamber of Commerce, Huntsville, Ont. P0A 1K0. Free maps at park office or Chamber of Commerce, Huntsville.

Mount Madawaska Ski Area
LOCATION: From Barry's Bay south 6 km on Hwy. 62.
LENGTH: About 30 km of interconnecting trails from base area.

The cross-country trails run from a downhill ski area base and pass through quite rugged terrain east of Algonquin Park with hills up to 122 m high. There are mixed woods, lakes, beaver ponds and many scenic lookouts. Lodge has ski rental and repairs, lessons, restaurant, licensed lounge, and four Adirondack type lean-to log shelters along trails. A cross-country ski weekend is held in March. Trail maps and lodging information from ski area. Box 130, Barry's Bay, Ont.

Purdy's Lodge
LOCATION: West of Alogonquin Park. 40 km north of Huntsville. 6.4 km east of Kearney on the Clam Lake Rd.
LENGTH: Travel time about 7 hr. to complete all main trails.

Wooded and rolling terrain. Wilderness trails range from easy to difficult. Small lodge, can accommodate 6. Home cooking. Open all winter. Trails broken but not groomed. Guiding available. Travel unlimited on unused logging roads. Nearby downhill ski operation at Echo Ridge. Ski rentals there.

Timberline Lodge
LOCATION: Kearney, west of Algonquin Park.

This lodge provides bring-your-own sleeping-bag dormitory accommodation and hearty meals for skiers planning trips on an extensive trail system in the area. This is a land of rolling, tree-clad hills and frozen lakes and rivers. It is good terrain for skiers and snowshoers of all abilities. Many marked trails and unlimited opportunity for bushwhacking in the wilderness. The Kearney area receives about 400 cm of snow each winter and there is consistently good skiing until April most years.

14 Haliburton

Frost Centre Trails
LOCATION: From Dorset south 11 km on Hwy. 35.
LENGTH: 25 km.

The Leslie M. Frost Natural Resources Centre is the former Dorset Ranger or Forest Technical School, located on 22 000 ha in the Haliburton Highlands south of Algonquin Park. Cross-country facilities include a practice and warm-up area, marked trails and map. Much of the centre has been opened to the public for demonstration and educational projects in resources management, recreation and education. Programs are for day visitors and groups that have arranged to stay in the 83-room residences. Demonstrations include a sawmill, maple syrup operation, winter deer range management, fur bearing animal management, lake and stream management, geology and trail planning for activities including cross-country skiing. For more detailed information contact the centre at Dorset, Ont. P0A 1E0 or phone (705) 766-2451.

Nordic Inn
LOCATION: From Dorset north 1.5 km on Hwy. 35.
LENGTH: Total of 16 km in 4 loops. Travel time about 5 hr. for all trails.

Trails are in rolling hardwood country. Yellow and Green trails are for beginners and intermediate skiers. Red trail, designed for experts and intermediate skiers, consists of several steep declines and uphills, including sharp turns. In centre of trail system is a deer wintering area. Warm-up and waxing hut. Night skiing on 2 km of lighted trail. Licensed dining room. Accommodation for up to 40 people. Also two motels at Dwight, 18 km to the north. Maps available at resort.

Haliburton Forest Reserve
LOCATION: Southwest of Algonquin Park. From West Guilford north 19.5 km on Kennisis Lake Rd.
LENGTH: 30 km of trails cleared, marked and mapped in 4000 ha area.

The Haliburton Forest and Wild Life Reserve Ltd. is a privately owned 260 sq. km area catering mainly to snowmobilers but with a sizable section now reserved for cross-country skiers. This wooded, hilly area has a snow season that usually lasts from late December to late April. Rugged country with almost unlimited possibilities for wilderness skiing.

This Kennisis L. region, about 241 km from Toronto, is forested mostly with beech, maple and other hardwoods. It is an area of rolling hills up to 137 m high and with good views. The Gull, Black, Hollow, Madawaska and York rivers radiate from the high ground. Ski trails follow numerous logging roads. There is a hunting cabin for lunch stops and a remote cabin for overnight trips.

Map available and skier should obtain topographic map, Haliburton 31 E/2 in 1:50,000 series. Wild area with some markings not clear so should carry map and compass. Most accommodation at lodge booked by snowmobilers but some skiers bring trailers or find lodging in towns as much as 32 km distant. Fees for trail use.

For information write the reserve, RR 1, Haliburton, Ont. K0M 1S0.

Lake Kashagawigamog Trail
LOCATION: Haliburton Village. Start at museum at north edge of village or at resorts on the North Kashagawigamog Rd.
LENGTH: 30 km of loop trails.

This series of trails, through rolling, wooded country, links nine lodges, inns and cottages west from Haliburton Village, north of the lake. Trails range from novice to expert. Most areas sheltered by hills or bush. Trails are maintained by the L. Kashagawigamog Tourist Association and the Haliburton Highlands Cross-Country Club. Trails used during Minden Winter Carnival in January, Haliburton Winter Carnival in February and the Woodland Ranch Ski Tour later the same month. Maps available. For more information contact Lake Kashagawigamog Tourist Association, Box 459, Haliburton, Ont. K0M 1S0.

Sir Sam's Inn
LOCATION: From Haliburton north 16 km on Hwy. 519.
LENGTH: 8 km.

The lodge, located on the shore of Eagle L., has groomed trails running through nearby woodlands. Accommodation, dining room and ski rentals.

Woodland Ranch
LOCATION: North of Minden. Northwest of Haliburton. From Carnarvon east on Hwy. 530, south on 25th Line then east on local access road.

There are groomed and marked trails on parts of this 2400 ha ranch in the Haliburton Highlands. Trails for all levels of skiers. Cookout shelters along trails. Lunch bar and lounge at base. Ski shop, rentals, waxing area, repairs, lessons. Trail fee. Riding stable operates during winter. Accommodation in local lodges and motels. For more information contact Woodland Ranch, RR 1, Haliburton, Ont. K0M 1S0 or phone (705) 754-2040.

Bon Echo Provincial Park
LOCATION: Southeast of Bancroft. From Cloyne go north 16 km on Hwy. 41 to parking lot.
LENGTH: 8 km (subject to expansion).

Loop trails of 3 and 5 km have been developed, mainly on the road system of this 6200 ha park, but trails may be expanded if there is demand. Terrain is wooded and the park includes lakes and rivers. Trails groomed, outdoor toilets. Snowmobile trails start from the same general area.

15 Peterborough – Kawarthas

Balsam Lake Provincial Park
LOCATION: Northwest of Fenelon Falls on shore of Balsam L. From Hwy. 48 take Balsam Lake Rd.
LENGTH: 5 km.

This trail, with a side loop and a short loop at the end, starts near the parking lot in a 400 ha park. Snowmobile trails start nearby and run on separate route in same area. Park is a mixture of woods and open areas.

Victoria Forest Trails
LOCATION: North of Fenelon Falls. On south side of Hwy. 503, 5.5 km west of Kinmount.
LENGTH: 8 km of loops.

The Ministry of Natural Resources has developed two loop trails of 3.2 and 4.8 km in the Victoria County Agreement Forest. The first loop covers relatively flat and heavily forested country while the second section runs through numerous clearings, passes a swampy area and includes more rolling country. Trails are marked with arrows, colored tape and ski signs. Map at start of trails. Parking, toilets.

Byrnell Golf Course Ski Trails
LOCATION: Fenelon Falls. From town go east 3 km on Hwy. 35A.
LENGTH: 16 km of loops.

A series of trails fans out from the chalet and restaurant at this ski area on a golf course. Groomed and packed trails for all levels. Lessons, rentals, waxing area and babysitting on weekends. Special rates for families, schools and large groups. For more information call (705) 887-2935.

Connemara Camp and Centre
LOCATION: Kawartha Lakes area. From Fenelon Falls north 27 km on Hwy. 121 to Galway Rd., east 14 km on Galway Rd. to Centre.
LENGTH: Loop trails ranging from 400 m to 8 km.

Trails primarily wooded, some over open, hilly pasture, some over lake. For all levels of skiers. Weekend program by reservation, instruction, lunch only, cookouts available. Group retreats, some overnight accommodation, natural marked trails. Weekday outdoor education sessions available for schools and youth groups. Snowbunny events for children. For brochure and maps, write Connemara Camp and Centre, c/o Bruce and Patti Fleury, 52 Mid Pines Rd., Scarborough, Ont. or at the Centre, RR 1, Kinmount, Ont.

Ski Bethany

LOCATION: West of Peterborough. From Bethany on Hwy. 7A go north 3.2 km on Conc. 11.
LENGTH: 3 km loop.

Bethany Ski Club, founded in 1927, is one of the oldest in Ontario. It is mainly a downhill resort, with a 116-metre high ski hill but club members report there have always been some cross-country skiers. Trail passes through cedar woods and is suitable for all abilities. Deer, small game and birds in area. Grooming, chalet, snack bar, cookout, waxing hut, instruction can be arranged. For information contact Bethany Ski Club Inc., Box 472, Peterborough, Ont.

Devil's Elbow

LOCATION: West of Peterborough. From Bethany village on Hwy. 7A go north 5 km on Conc. 11.
LENGTH: Loop trails of 2.5 km (approx. one-half hour travel) and 6 km (approx. 1 1/4 hours travel).

Cross-country trails located north of downhill slopes in forested hill and valley area. Club has rentals, instruction, trail grooming, food and snowshoeing facilities. Map available at the area. For further information call (705) 277-2012.

Cavendish Ski Area

LOCATION: From Peterborough north 60 km on Hwy. 507. Parking on west side, opposite Beaver Lake Rd. turnoff and at Red Lion Inn, 100 m south.
LENGTH: 6 km.

Ski area was developed in 1975 by four Toronto high school students working with an Opportunities for Youth grant and cooperation of landowners, the Coppys and Strongs. Traverses meadows, marshes, reforested areas, hardwood and mixed forest with stands of giant white pines. Generally rolling country with easy trails and advanced routes with some rugged sections. Three trails marked with colored arrows, paint and tape. Skiers are cautioned to expect the Coppy's horses on the trail and to give them the right of way. Keep gates closed and treat the private property with respect. Red Lion Inn caters to skiers with rooms, meals, bar, washrooms, ski rentals and trail maps. Information and map from Glen Campbell, 55 Melrose Ave., Toronto, Ont. M5M 1Y6.

Ganaraska Trail

LOCATION: A partially completed 500 km trail through Southern Ontario from Port Hope to Glen Huron.

The Ganaraska was started in 1967 after the Bruce Trail was finished and first pushed north from Port Hope on L. Ontario. In 1970 the trail association was formed to continue the new route until it joined the Bruce at Glen Huron, about 16 km south of Collingwood. It was designed as a hiking trail but much of it is usable for cross-country skiing and snowshoeing.

The route is through pleasant rural land. In the Port Hope area there are pine forests; the Kawarthas have the scenic ruggedness of the Canadian Shield; west of Orillia there are sand hills; near Midland the Wye Marsh Wildlife Centre and the Glen Huron area includes a section by the Mad River valley. A branch trail passes the historic Ste. Marie reconstructed Jesuit mission of four centuries ago. Trail marked with brown arrows on white, but maps necessary. Write: Ganaraska Trail Assn., Box 1136, Barrie, Ont. L4M 5E2.

Kawartha Ski Tour Trail

LOCATION: Kawartha Lakes region north of Peterborough. Trail runs between Apsley and Buckhorn.
LENGTH: 59 km in three major sections with small side loops.

This is the scene, in the middle of each February, of the Kawartha Tour, a major event preceding the Canadian Ski Marathon. Tour runs from Apsley south and west to Buckhorn, 33 km north of Peterborough. Trail is in three main sections: Apsley to Haultain (23 km, 4 hr.), Haultain to Deer Bay (20 km, 3 hr.) and Deer Bay to Buckhorn (16 km, 2 1/2 hr.). This is a very scenic wilderness area and trail officials advise skiers to travel in parties with map, compass and proper touring equipment. Conditions are sometimes rugged and Haultain to Deer Bay section has considerable ice travel. Apsley to Haultain section has some difficult hills. In general a mostly wooded trail with some open areas. Good possibilities for spotting wildlife. Trail marked with orange signs. Maps from Kawartha Nordic Ski Club Inc., Box 1371, Peterborough, Ont. Information on the tour and lodging from Kawartha Tourist Assn., 393 Water St., Peterborough.

McKay Lake Trail

LOCATION: Apsley.
LENGTH: 5 km (about 1 hr.).

Trail in wooded terrain, starts from same point as a snowmobile trail. Start is near motel and restaurant. This trail is less than 1 km from start of the annual Kawartha Tour, held each year in mid-February from Apsley to Buckhorn. Accommodation information from Apsley Tourist Assn., Box 383, Apsley, Ont. K0L 1A0.

Silent Lake Park

LOCATION: North of Peterborough. From Apsley north 19.5 km on Hwy. 28.
LENGTH: 38 km in loops for varying abilities: 2 to 6 hr. trips.

Silent Lake Provincial Park has a series of groomed trails through a wooded, wilderness area around the lake. All water crossings are bridged. A 6 km trail suitable for novices or families has only gradual downhill runs. A 12 km route requires ability to sidestep up hills and snowplow down. The 20 km trail is for experienced touring skiers and winds around the lake with considerable variations in terrain and scenery. There are old roads and trails, open sections, flats and hills, beaver ponds, mature balsam and white birch stands along the way. The trail finishes with a climb, then a downhill run to the parking lot. Map at start of trail. Lodging information from Apsley Tourist Assn., Box 383, Apsley, Ont. K0L 1A0.

Selwyn Conservation Area

LOCATION: On shore of Chemung L., 18 km north of Peterborough. Take Highways 28 and 507 through Selwyn then left on Conc. 12 and north on access road.

Cross-country skiing has been established by local skiers in this 31 ha conservation area. A loop trail winds through woods and open areas and along the beach on the irregular lake shoreline.

Warsaw Caves

LOCATION: From Peterborough northeast on County Rd. 4, north of town of Warsaw.
LENGTH: 10 km.

This conservation area is based around an extensive collection of caves and kettles (potholes) scoured out of the limestone by the melting Laurentide ice cap. Skiers use a system of trails also used for hiking during warmer months. Area of considerable geological interest. Mixture of mature forest and reforested limestone plains. For information and map contact Otonabee Region Conservation Authority, 727 Lansdowne St. W., Peterborough, Ont. K9J 1Z2 or phone (705) 745-5791.

Jackson Park

LOCATION: On both sides of Jackson Creek, north of Parkhill Rd., Peterborough.

A short series of interlocking trails runs alongside and crosses Jackson Creek above and below a dam. Trails also cross small, frozen streams and marsh and circle a pond. There are parking lots on both sides of Jackson Creek with access from Parkhill Rd. on the west side and Fairburn St. on the east side of the creek.

Old Orchard Park

LOCATION: From Peterborough go east 3 km on Hwy. 7 then north 1.5 km on access road.
LENGTH: 20 km of loop trails.

Groomed, tracked and marked trails for all levels of skiers on 128 ha of varied terrain. Mixture of open and wooded areas with hills. Rentals, instruction, waxing area, downhill skiing, skating, tobogganing, sleigh rides, snack bar. Trails are used for competition by local high schools. For more information write Old Orchard Park, RR 7, Peterborough, Ont. or phone (705) 745-5251.

Riverview Park and Zoo

LOCATION: Just north of Peterborough on Hwy. 28 at dam and pumphouse on Otonabee R.

The Peterborough Utilities Commission has a small park with bird and animal enclosures along the river banks. There is a short trail around the area. Skating day and night. For information call (705) 745-4615, ext. 24.

Squirrel Creek Conservation Area

LOCATION: South of Peterborough. From Hwy. 28 go east and north for about 3 km on County Rd. 28 (Wallace Point Rd.).
LENGTH: 3 km loop.

This roughly circular trail wanders near Squirrel Creek, then along the edge of the Otonabee R. before returning to the parking lot near the east side of Wallace Point Rd. Area along creek is marshy. Conservation area is 110 ha. For map and more information contact the Otonabee Region Conservation Authority, 727 Lansdowne St. W., Peterborough, Ont. K9J 1Z2 or phone (705) 745-5791.

Northumberland County Forest
LOCATION: From Cobourg, 13 km north of Hwy. 401 on Hwy. 45; turn left at Beagle Club Rd.
LENGTH: Loop trails of 17.8 km. Graded beginner to intermediate.

Trails wind through wooded, hilly terrain and pine plantations with views of Oak Ridges glacial moraine. Downhill ski club also located in the county forest. Park at Beagle Club Rd. parking lot to avoid traffic of downhill skiers and snowmobilers. Maps available on site or from Ministry of Natural Resources, 322 Kent St. W., Lindsay, Ont. K9V 2T9 or phone (705) 324-6121.

Swiss Chalet Farms
LOCATION: North of Grafton and east of Cobourg. From Hwy. 401 at Interchange 84 go north on Aird St. 400 m then right on access road to farm.
LENGTH: 5 km loop.

This ski trail is located at a resort of 280 ha. Route runs through farmland. Indoor pool, sauna, whirlpool and games room.

Seymour Conservation Area
LOCATION: Just south of Campbellford on east side of Hwy. 30.
LENGTH: 6 km.

Two loop trails run through 80 ha area in generally open limestone plains and upland wooded drumlin. Requires moderate skiing ability. Skating rink in old limestone quarry. Ski shelters and cookout areas. Maintained trail starts at parking lot, where a map is posted. Pocket map and more information from Lower Trent Region Conservation Authority, Box 180, Frankford, Ont. K0K 2C0 or phone (613) 398-6123.

Proctor Conservation Area
LOCATION: North end of Brighton off Hwy. 30.
LENGTH: 2.5 km conservation area trail, which leads to 4 km Brighton Lions Club trail.

Loop trail starts from parking lot at west side of Younge St. (Hwy. 30) and runs north, at points beside the Butler Creek. It crosses open grassland, and forests of maple, cottonwood, beech, cedar and some abandoned orchards. Two steep hills with switchbacks, which demand good skiing ability. Bridge over creek. Area for off-trail skiing in back part of 36 ha property where there are open woodlots and ravines. Site of Proctor House Museum, where there is plowed parking lot. The conservation authority trail is signed with red markers and from two points on it you can pick up 4 km Lions Club trail with blue markers, which crosses private land. For map and more information contact Lower Trent Region Conservation Authority, Box 180, Frankford, Ont. K0K 2C0 or phone (613) 398-6123.

Presqu'ile Provincial Park
LOCATION: From Brighton south 3 km.
LENGTH: 7 km loop.

The trail runs through a wooded, fairly level area known for its wildlife. The peninsula, which juts into L. Ontario, is a bird watchers' haven – 293 species of birds have been sighted there. It also holds a number of animals. They include red squirrels, eastern cottontails, red fox, hares and deer. The peninsula is a limestone island left by glacial retreat of about 10 000 years ago combined with a series of sand and gravel spits. It is covered by forests, marshes, sand dunes, abandoned farms and cobble beaches. The point was once a refuge harbor and the lighthouse is still a landmark. In 1955 it became a provincial park. For brochure and more information contact: Ministry of Natural Resources, 1 Richmond Blvd., Napanee, Ont. K7R 3S3 or phone (613) 354-2173.

Goodrich-Loomis Conservation Area
LOCATION: North of Brighton. From Hwy. 401 north about 5 km on Hwy 30 then west on Conc. 7 following conservation authority signs.
LENGTH: Loop trails of 8 km.

Three trails of 1.5 to 4.6 km are located in this area, which is forested with cedar, pine, hemlock, beech and poplar. The main feature of the 180 ha area is the Codrington Esker, a high gravel ridge which gives a good view of the surrounding countryside. Cold Creek flows through area and the trails cross it on bridges. Trails groomed, shelters and cookout areas. Conservation authority holds family ski day early each February. Map on display at area. Pocket maps and more information from Lower Trent Region Conservation

Authority, Box 180, Frankford, Ont. or phone (613) 398-6123.

16 Belleville Area

Quinte-Hastings Recreational Trail

This major hiking and ski trail crosses a large section of Eastern Ontario as it wanders for about 200 km from L. Ontario to just south of Algonquin Park.

The trail starts near Sandbanks Provincial Park, passes Trenton and strikes north through farm, bush, lake and river country to the scenic area near the south tip of Algonquin. The trail ends at Lake St. Peter Provincial Park.

During the winter much of the trail is used by snowmobiles so the trail association has established additional routes on or near the main pathway for cross-country skiers. These have parking areas signalled with orange signs and have a supply of maps and brochures.

Since much of the skiing is on private land the association urges skiers "to leave no other signs of your presence than ski tracks." Trails are maintained by club members with financial assistance from Ministry of Natural Resources. For maps and further information about the trail and the club contact: Quinte-Hastings Recreational Trail Assn. Inc., Box 1333, Belleville, Ont., K8N 5J1.

Sophiasburg Trails

LOCATION: On Hwy. 14 opposite Mountain View Airport about 15 km south of Belleville.

This trail follows a large bluff overlooking the Bay of Quinte. There is a long hill at the start of the trail which demands downhill skills.

Loyalist Trail

LOCATION: Start at parking lot west of William R. Kirk School, West Bridge St., Belleville.
LENGTH: 8 km.

Trail runs as loop between school and Loyalist Community College and is marked with blue metal strips at eye level. Also white directional signs with skier symbol. Maps and more information about trails and lodging from Quinte-Hastings Recreational Trail Assn.

Sidney Trail

LOCATION: North of Belleville. Access points at: Pine Hill Cres. on Hwy. 62, 4.8 km west of Foxboro; Gallivan Rd. at Hwy. 14, 8 km northwest of Foxboro; southeast corner of Oak Hills Flying Club field, between Conc. 6 and 8; Conc. 6 and Fish and Game Club Rd., 1.6 km northeast of Frankford.

This is part of a hiking trail suitable for cross-country skiing and is a linear trail, not a loop. It is marked with orange metal strips and orange symbols of a hiker. Maps and more information about trails and lodging from Quinte-Hastings Recreational Trail Assn.

Kuglin Trail

LOCATION: North of Belleville. Start at Kuglin Farm on Hwy. 14, 4.8 km west of Foxboro.
LENGTH: 13 km.

This trail runs as a loop through the Kuglin and neighboring Ketcheson farms. Marked with blue metal strips at eye level and white directional signs with skier symbol. Maps and more information about trails and lodging from Quinte-Hastings Recreational Trail Assn.

Chatterton-Wallbridge Ski Area

LOCATION: About 15 km north of Belleville. Located on north side of County Rd. 5 midway between Foxboro and Frankford.
LENGTH: Three loops of 2, 2.1 and 2.6 km.

These trails traverse drumlin country near the Oak hills. Generally need intermediate ability including hill manoeuvres for the sharp bends in the trails. Land includes open and forested stretches with beaver pond in middle of the area. Warm up area at sugar shack. Parking.

Frink Centre Trail

LOCATION: About 16 km north of Belleville. From Hwy. 37 at Plainfield Children's Home turn east on Thurlow Twp. Conc. 6 for 2 km.
LENGTH: 2.6 km loop.

This short trail was developed by the Quinte-Hastings Trail Assn. with the Hastings County Board of Education, the Moira River Conservation Authority and the Ministry of Natural Resources. It passes through a mixture of open and wooded areas and is used during the winter for school outings. Parking.

Goodfellow Trails

LOCATION: North of Belleville 20 km. From Hwy. 37 at Plainfield take Scuttlehole Rd. across Moira R.

LENGTH: Three loops of 2.75, 3.75 and 4.5 km.

This series of trails on the east side of the river has two relatively easy trails through farmland. They have travel times of from 15 to 30 minutes. The red trail, which takes about an hour to complete, is more difficult. It passes through the Moira Karst geological area where there are many sinkholes and caves in the limestone. There are also some of the largest sugar maples in Hastings County. Parking.

Vanderwater Conservation Area

LOCATION: From Belleville north 25 km on Hwy. 37 to Thomasburg then east 2 km on county access road.
LENGTH: 13 km of loop trails.

Five trails, ranging from .7 to 5.5 km, start at parking lot. Marked and groomed trails run along the Moira R. and climb a nearby ridge. In some places they follow park roads. Picnic tables, enclosed shelter, toilets, fireplaces and natural spring.

Camp Inn Trail

LOCATION: From Hwy. 62, 800 m east on Concession 12 of Huntingdon Twp. (Quin-Mo-Lac Rd.).
LENGTH: 13 km

This loop trail just south of Moira L. is operated by Jamie Campkin's Camp Inn and the Quinte-Hastings Recreational Trail Assn. Snack bar and lounge. Maps and more information about trails and lodging from Quinte-Hastings Recreational Trail Assn.

Supper of the Lamb Trails

LOCATION: North of Belleville. From Tweed go north on Hwy. 37 for 5 km to Supper of the Lamb Restaurant on the east side of the road and stop in public parking lot.
LENGTH: 17.5 km of loops.

Three trails, a low-intermediate loop of 2.5 km or 20 min., an intermediate run of 5 km or 45 min. and an advanced trail of 10 km or an average of 90 min. fan out from the parking lot. Area is scenic Shield country with beaver ponds along the creeks. Trails groomed, shelter and bridges. Restaurant open on weekends and some evenings. Trails maintained by the Moira Valley Nordic Ski Club, Moira Valley Conservation Authority, Ministry of Natural Resources and the restaurant. Maps at the restaurant.

Henry's Ski Farm Association

LOCATION: North of Belleville. From Tweed go north on Hwy. 37 to edge of town then east on Hastings Rd. 39 or 5.5 km to 90-degree left curve where you turn south (right) for 800 m, crossing Clare R. and going through hamlet of Bogart. At top of Bogart hill head southeast (left) and continue to take left fork at all junctions for next 5.5 km to the farm.
LENGTH: 25 km of loops.

This area has six trails ranging from 1 to 10 km on undulating farmland with some wooded areas. Rentals, instruction, guide, home-cooked meals at the farm, sauna, fireplace, map at area. Trails maintained. For more information write Henry Myyra, RR 3, Tweed, Ont. or phone (613) 478-3227.

Sandbanks-Outlet Beach Areas

LOCATION: From Picton southwest about 16 km on County Roads 10 and 11.
LENGTH: 16 km loop at Outlet.

Two neighboring provincial parks have cross-country skiing in a scenic region along the shore of L. Ontario. Outlet Beach is a 270 ha natural environment park on a wide sandbar across the mouth of a large bay. To the northwest about 3 km are the long, high dunes of Sandbanks Park. Historic sites in the area include the Mariners' Lighthouse Museum, southeast of Milford, the Early Settlers' Museum, east of Waupoos and The Carrying Place Indian Portage. For information on the parks and area contact: Ministry of Natural Resources, 1 Richmond Blvd, Napanee, Ont. K7R 3S3 or phone (613) 354-2173.

Macaulay Mountain Conservation Area

LOCATION: From Hwy. 33 on eastern outskirts of Picton go southeast on County Rd. 8 (Union St.) to access road. Trail starts near recreational shelter.
LENGTH: Loop trail of 8 km. Travel time 1 hr. Extensive touring possibilities on plateau.

Trail runs along and below an escarpment with a maximum drop of 30-46 metres. Slope varies, providing a gentle grade at the eastern edge. A mature forest exists along the escarpment. Open grassland predominates in lower areas, north of the escarpment. The plateau to the south of the escarpment is predominantly flat terrain covered with red cedar. Generally, the trail is not too difficult, except for a small portion which is particularly steep. The escarpment portion of the trail is laid through a mature climax forest including some Carolinian species and a stand of mature hemlock. The slope trail provides views of Picton Bay and the surrounding area. For lodging information, write Quinte's Isle Tourist Assn., 116 Main St., Picton, Ont. Maps at shelter, 9 A.M. to 5 P.M.

17 Kingston – Rideau Area

Arden Conservation Area
LOCATION: West side of Arden, just south of Hwy. 7.
LENGTH: 5 km of loops.

This 94 ha park has trails running to the south and west sides of Cedar L., just west of the village. Trails include three loops and a connecting section in scenic hilly and wooded country. Trails marked and groomed, picnic tables, shelter, barbecues, snowshoeing. For brochure-map and more information contact Napanee Region Conservation Authority, 174 Robinson St., Napanee, Ont. K7R 2S4 or phone (613) 354-3312.

Baker's Valley Trails
LOCATION: On Hwy. 7 northwest of Kingston. From Kaladar go east 20 km on Hwy 10. North of Arden.
LENGTH: 21 km.

This cross-country resort has bush trails in hilly, wooded country. Routes for all levels of ability. Free instruction is a feature of the resort. Groomed trails, rentals, shelter on trail, picnic area and snack bar in chalet. There is a slalom run on a nearby hill for skiers who want to try their skills at downhill runs on skinny skis. The area is inhabited by such wildlife as deer, wolf, owls and racoons, which have a den along one of the trails. Map at area. For more information contact Ross Baker, RR 1, Arden, Ont. or phone (613) 335-5547 or phone 478-2632.

Balahack Mountain Park
LOCATION: North of Napanee. From Tamworth go east 6.5 km on Mountain Rd.
LENGTH: About 50 km of loop trails.

The park is on 560 ha of hilly, wooded country, which shelters a resident deer herd in the winter. There is a network of nine loop trails for beginner through intermediate level skiers. Trails marked and groomed. Lakes to explore when the ice is safe. Chalet open on weekends with health food plus hamburgers, soup, sandwiches, etc. Chalet has fireplaces, waxing area, dance floor and is available for rental. Instruction, ski and snowshoe rentals, guide service, ice fishing. Sleigh rides can be arranged. Loppet planned. Maps available. Trail is maintained by owner and Napanee Cross-Country Ski Club. For more information write the owner, Mike Kouri, RR 2, Tamworth, Ont. K0K 3G0.

Depot Lakes Conservation Area
LOCATION: From Verona north on Hwy. 38 then west on Snider Rd. for a total of about 10 km.
LENGTH: 10 km.

A series of seven loop trails run off a main route around the west sides of Second and Third Depot Lakes. Trails are in a 1328 ha hilly and wooded park in Shield country. Parking, picnic tables, barbecues, shelter, toilets, groomed trails, snowshoeing and tobogganing. Wildlife and rugged scenery. Area covered by topographic map 31 C/10, second edition. Map on brochure and more information from Napanee Region Conservation Authority, 174 Robinson St., Napanee, Ont. K7R 2S4 or phone (613) 354-3312.

Gould Lake Conservation Area
LOCATION: From Sydenham northeast 10.5 km. Follow signs 35.5 km northeast of Kingston.
LENGTH: 5 km of trails within the Rideau Trail System.

The trails traverse glacial land forms, mostly through woods. The area is used by skiers of all ability but is quite popular with the more advanced ones. This 600 ha conservation area is a wilderness land. A large number of porcupines, beavers, raccoons and the occasional white tail deer inhabit the area as do numerous bird species. Accommodation in the Kingston area. Contact the Kingston Chamber of Commerce, 209 Ontario St., Kingston, Ont. Trail guide available free of charge from the Cataraqui Region Conservation Authority Office, RR 1, Glenburnie, Ont. K0H 1S0.

Lemoine Point Conservation Area
LOCATION: From Kingston travel to the end of Front Rd. (Follow Airport signs.)
LENGTH: 4 km loop trail. Maximum travel time 1 hr.

The trails are located on a 135 ha conservation area with a kilometre of shoreline on L. Ontario. The trail goes across a flat, open field, then enters a wooded area covering an elevated portion of the shoreline. Can be used by all levels of skiers. Accommodation in the Kingston area. Contact the Kingston Chamber of Commerce, 209 Ontario St., Kingston, Ont. Trail guide available free of charge from the Cataraqui Region Conservation Authority Office, RR 1, Glenburnie, Ont. K0H 1S0.

Little Cataraqui Creek Conservation Area
LOCATION: From Exit 102 on Hwy. 401 at Kingston, go north 1.6 km on County Rd. 10.
LENGTH: Loop trails of about 9 km. Travel time 2 to 3 hr.

This trail system traverses rolling terrain in a 400 ha conservation area. Some trails go through the woods while others cross open fields. For skiers of all ability. Natural skating rink with a small changing shelter. Snowshoeing. Accommodation in the Kingston area. Contact the Kingston Chamber of Commerce, 209 Ontario St., Kingston, Ont. Trail map free from the Cataraqui Region Conservation Authority Office, RR 1, Glenburnie, Ont. K0H 1S0.

Rideau Trail
LOCATION: Kingston to Ottawa via Rideau Canal.
LENGTH: 400 km hiking trail with 210 km suitable for cross-country skiing.

The Rideau is one of Ontario's four major hiking trails and parts of it with no steep sections are suitable for skiing though they are not groomed. Trail starts on L. Ontario shore in the marshes of the Little Cataraqui R. and winds north to the Chaudière Falls near Parliament Hill. Terrain ranges from serene pastoral to rugged Eastern Ontario wilderness. Wildlife and many historic sites. Follows route of the Rideau Canal, built in 19th century.

From start, trail heads north to Sydenham, then plunges into the wild country of Frontenac Park, an area of rocks and beaver dams. It winds through the Rideau Lakes region, along the Tay R. and past Perth, Smith Falls and Merrickville. To north it enters Ottawa from southwest past Bells Corner and joins Ottawa R. near Britannia Bay. Camp and build fires only with land owners' permission. Many access points from roads. Trail marked with orange triangles, side trails with blue. Like its sister trails the Rideau was built by interested citizens. Club holds ski seminars, clinics, outings. Must join club to get maps. Write Rideau Trail Assn., Box 15, Kingston, Ont. K7L 4V6.

18 St. Lawrence Valley

Brockville Cross-Country Ski Trails
LOCATION: At west end of city between Hwy. 401, Lynn Rd. and CNR line. Parking at west end of Central Ave.
LENGTH: Five interconnecting trails totalling 9.5 km.

Trails for novices and more advanced skiers range through wooded country, which is sometimes very hilly. At some places the trails cross a creek. Shelter with fire box. Grooming and marking by Brockville Cross-Country Ski Club. Site of annual Ookpik Carnival and ski marathon. Map available from local sports shops and Brockville Recreation Dept., City Hall, King St., Brockville, Ont.

Buells Creek Conservation Area
LOCATION: From Hwy. 401 at north edge of Brockville follow Hwy. 29 north 5 km then 2.5 km east on Centennial Rd. to entrance on north side.

The 526 ha tract is operated by the Cataraqui Conservation Authority, RR 1, Glenburnie, Ont., which publishes a brochure on the area. It is not specifically developed as a cross-country ski area but can be used as such. There is already a hiking trail from the northeast corner around the west side of the reservoir, which occupies half the area. The land is mostly flat and forms part of the Smiths Falls Limestone Plain. Low ridges north and west of pond were formed after last ice age 10000 years ago.

Wildlife includes white-tailed deer, beaver, muskrat, porcupine and small mammals. Early and late in ski season waterfowl start to gather at pond.

Charleston Lake Provincial Park
LOCATION: 14.5 km north of Lansdowne, just off County Rd. 3, 22.5 km northeast of Gananoque.
LENGTH: Trails of 5, 6.5, 10 km, graded beginner to intermediate. Trip time 1 to 2 hr.

Charleston Lake is a 760 ha natural environment park. It is situated on the edge of a narrow extension of the Canadian Shield, with fields, wooded valleys, open ridgetops, swamps, marshes and forest. Wildlife includes porcupine, ruffed grouse and red fox. Winter birdwatchers may find blue jays, white-breasted nuthatches, black-capped chickadees and woodpeckers. Trail grooming. Two warm-up cabins located along the trails with stoves and firewood. A toboggan, first aid kit and blankets are provided for emergency use. Two snowshoe trails. Trail brochure available free from park or Ministry of Natural Resources District Office in Brockville. 1:50,000 topographical maps of the Charleston Lake area are as follows: Westport 31 C/9, Brockville 31 B/12, Gananoque 31 C/8 and Mallorytown 31 B/5.

Maitlands Trails

LOCATION: From Hwy. 2 at town of Maitland. For main entrance to orange trail go north 400 m on County Rd. 15. Entrance on west side of road opposite Esso station. Parking. Other parts of trail start in town.
LENGTH: 30 km. 3 loop trails plus crossovers. Longest (orange) trail is 10 km with average travel time of 1-1½ hr.

Wooded terrain with gentle slopes. Rated for all levels of skiers. Rentals in sports shop in Brockville, 6.2 km west of Maitland. Ski school Saturday mornings, mid-January to mid-February. Maps available at White House Motel on Hwy. 2 and at Esso station. Orienteering held here in fall and inter-school ski races during winter. Trails were started in 1973 by Maitland Trails, Box 89, Maitland, Ont. K0E 1P0. For accommodation information contact Brockville Chamber of Commerce.

1000 Islands Nordic Ski Trails

LOCATION: Between Kingston and Brockville. From 1000 Islands Bridge east 4 km on 1000 Islands Parkway. Trail entrance beside Caiger's Lodge, just east of Rockport.
LENGTH: Series of loops and interconnecting trails totalling 40 km.

Network of trails is just north of the St. Lawrence R. between the 1000 Islands Parkway and Hwy. 401. Runs through mainly wooded Canadian Shield type terrain with some open areas. Trails are marked and groomed by the local ski association. Ski patrol. Base is at Caiger's Lodge where trail fees are paid and first aid station is located. Rentals available in Brockville and Kingston. Lodging at Caiger's Lodge. Map available. For more information write: 1000 Islands Nordic Ski Trails, Box 36, Landsdowne, Ont. K0E 1L0.

Sand Lake Mountain Trail

LOCATION: Bordering Sand L. on Maberly Hwy. at northern edge of Westport.
LENGTH: 5 km loop. About 45 min. travel time.

This trail, maintained by the Upper Rideau Ski Club, runs through hilly, mainly wooded country around Sand L. It is best to ski the circular route in a counterclockwise direction. Trail is rated at beginner to intermediate difficulty. Lodging in Westport. For map and further information contact the Upper Rideau Ski Club in Westport at (613) 273-2839.

Summerstown Station Forest

LOCATION: From Cornwall go east 13 km on Summerstown Station Rd.
LENGTH: 26 km of loops.

This network of trails is located in a provincial government forest and is maintained by the cross-country section of the Cornwall Ski Club. Trails groomed, shelters, maps at trail. The terrain is about two-thirds wooded and includes some small hills. Trails rated for beginners and intermediates.

19 Lower Ottawa Valley

Ottawa Area

The National Capital Commission lists five distinct cross-country ski areas in Ottawa plus another in Hull. In addition, there is a large cross-country and downhill ski resort at Camp Fortune, just north of Hull. Area residents can get a brochure with sketch maps of the areas by phoning the NCC (613) 992-4321. Skiing areas range from parkland in the middle of Ottawa to creeks and swamps on the outskirts. In addition there is skiing on the Rideau R. when ice conditions are safe, along some parts of the Ottawa R. shoreline and on parts of the bikeway.

Stony Swamp Ski Trails

LOCATION: Access at several points in Bells Corners, Nepean Twp., west of Ottawa. Major access from Cedarview Rd. near Bell High School.
LENGTH: About 30 km of trails, mostly in loops, ranging up to 17 km.

Stony Swamp is under the care of three organizations: the National Capital Commission owns the land, the Ministry of Natural Resources manages the land and is planting trees and the Nepean Parks and Recreation Dept. has co-ordinated and extensively studied the development of ski trails since 1973. Parks officials feel it is a rare example of a major cross-country ski area so near a large urban area. Some waxing and ski instruction is offered. Maps at parking lot. Some races.

From built-up area trails wander south and west into undeveloped land, skirting the occasional road. Terrain is mostly level and there are fields, cedar bogs, pine barrens, coniferous and deciduous forests and beaver ponds. Area is a bird haven and animals include fox, squirrel, skunk, beaver and porcupine. Old Quarry Trail passes exposed rocks 450 million years old and fossil sea shells that can be seen in the rocks. Other trails pass beaver cuttings and demonstration plots for forestry studies. Sketch map on NCC Winter Trails folder and information from Nepean Parks and Recreation Dept., 1701 Woodroffe Ave., Ottawa, Ont. K2G 1W2.

Green Creek — Mer Bleue Trails
LOCATION: Centred around Blackburn Hamlet on eastern edge of Ottawa.
LENGTH: About 30 km.

Just 9 km from the Parliament Buildings, a long network of trails ranges through parkway belt land largely following the Green Creek inland from its mouth at the Ottawa R. near Lower Duck L. The trail passes west of Blackburn Village, then follows the creek as it swings eastward into the large swamp area known as Mer Bleue. The trail makes several loops along the way and passes the Magnetic Laboratory of the Dept. of Energy, Mines and Resources before heading further south across Borthwick Cr. There is access and parking at the toboggan slide at Orleans Rd. and at several other points including two places on the dead-end extension of Ridge Rd. east of County Rd. 42. Sketch map with fair detail on National Capital Commission Winter Trails folder.

Hogs Back and Vincent Massey Parks
LOCATION: On east bank of Rideau R. north and south of Heron Ave, Ottawa.

Two modest trails form loops along the river bank and inland. From here a skier can travel further afield along the river bank using the bikeway system.

Pine Grove
LOCATION: Just south of Ottawa city limits, east and west of Hwy. 31 near Kempark and Canadian Forces Base Leitrim.

These are two loop trails in National Capital Commission greenbelt forest at the city's edge. The small loop of about 5 km starts at Capital Golf Gardens just north of Kempark. A much more extensive network of seven trails is located north of CFB Leitrim and touches several roads, including Davidson Rd., and Conroy Rd. Main access points off Davidson Rd. west of Hawthorne and Leitrim Rd. east of Hawthorne. Map on NCC Winter Trails folder.

Pinhey Forest
LOCATION: Nepean Twp. Starts at Sportsplex on Woodroffe Ave. just north of Slack Rd.
LENGTH: 6 km.

Two trail loops have been developed north and south of Slack Rd. in area that is mainly forested but has some open fields. Surrounding area partially developed. Maps at Sportsplex and on National Capital Commission Winter Trails folder.

Shirleys Bay Trails
LOCATION: Shirleys Bay on Deschenes Lake on Ottawa R. just west of Ottawa. Take Hwy. 17B to Rifle Range Rd. then drive to parking lot at the shore.
LENGTH: 6 km of loops.

The National Capital Commission has a double loop of 1.5 and 4.5 km trails on slightly hilly land between the highway and the shore.

"Y" Ski and Outdoor Centre
LOCATION: From Ottawa west 16 km on Queensway, north 6.4 km on Hwy. 17, turn right, 90 m to Regional Rd. 8, turn right again towards Ottawa R., 6.4 km to ski centre.
LENGTH: Loop trails of 3.2 km.

58 ha of wooded area. 2.5 m wide trails on flat and hilly terrain. Trails groomed. Weekend operation with focus on instruction, novice to intermediate levels. Snowshoeing, skating, tobogganing, sleigh rides. Groups may rent facilities for parties. Dining hall and chalet. Bunk house accommodation. Bring sleeping bag. For information, write Ottawa YM-YWCA, 180 Argyle Ave., Ottawa, Ont. Registration Office.

Baxter Conservation Area
LOCATION: South of Ottawa, from Kars on Rideau R. south 4 km on Regional Rd. 13.
LENGTH: 3.5 km of loops plus open areas and river.

This 64 ha conservation area has two loop trails plus potential for more skiing on old fields, through wooded areas and on the frozen Rideau R., which can offer skiing for 5 km in both directions. Ice conditions should be checked with local officials for safety. Skiing is suitable for beginners and families. There are cookout areas and ski clinics at certain times. On Sundays from mid-January to mid-March the interpretive centre is open and there are films, family cookouts, ski and snowshoe races and guided nature hikes. Maps at area. For more information contact Rideau Valley Conservation Authority, Box 599, Manotick, Ont. or phone (613) 692-3571.

Rideau Trail Association Ski Area
LOCATION: Northwest of Kemptville. From North Gower on Hwy. 16 go west on Regional Rd. 4 for 14 km.
LENGTH: 10 km loops.

The trail forms a figure 8 through mixed bush in the scenic Rideau Valley area. Suitable for all levels of skiers. Warm-up building, which can be used as lunch stop. Trail maintained by volunteers from the association.

Tay Valley Club Trail
LOCATION: From western edge of Perth the trail runs south to Murphy's Point Provincial Park.
LENGTH: 30 km or about 3 hrs. one way. In addition, there are loops of 1 – 10 km along trail.

The Tay Valley Cross-Country Ski Club trail runs mainly through rolling, wooded countryside, away from built-up areas. It crosses Rideau Hiking Trail at two points. Terrain varies from flat near Perth to more difficult about two-thirds of the way south, near the clubhouse. Skiers are warned to check ice conditions when crossing lakes and streams. Ski club has plowed parking lots at both ends of trail and at clubhouse where there are wood cookstoves and washrooms. Trails are double-track set and groomed during season. Tay Valley Loppet ski tour and race is held in mid-January. For trail map and information contact Tay Valley Cross-Country Ski Club, Box 275, Perth, Ont. or Tay Sports Centre in Perth.

Murphy's Point Provincial Park
LOCATION: About 20 km south of Perth. From Hwy. 7 in town go south on County Road 1, then west on Elm Grove Rd. to park.
LENGTH: 15 km of loops (about half on unplowed park roads).

This summer campground becomes a cross-country ski area in winter. Groomed ski trails follow park road system and nature trails. There is also a narrow, ungroomed hiking trail for more experienced skiers. Terrain is rolling and covered with mixed deciduous and coniferous forest. Ministry of Natural Resources warns that ice conditions can become unsafe in areas near some of the trails: the end of Hogg Bay where the creek flows in and at the mouth of the bay. Also ice along the shoreline can thaw during mild periods. For more information on the park write: Murphy's Point Provincial Park, RR 5, Perth, Ont. K7H 3C7, or phone (613) 267-5060.

Bass Lake Lodge Trails
LOCATION: Rideau Ferry, between Perth and Lombardy.

The Rideau Cross-Country Ski Club has three loop trails on property of a summer lodge and fishing resort. Terrain is partly wooded with some gentle hills. Rated at beginner to intermediate ability. It takes about 1 1/2 hr. to complete the trails under average conditions. Map at trail head. Food and shelter at the lodge. Snowmobiling. Accommodation at Rideau Ferry Inn at village of Rideau Ferry.

Lanark Ski Trails
LOCATION: From Perth southwest 10 km on County Rd. 1 and the Elm Grove Rd.
LENGTH: 3 trails of 1.6, 3.2 and 3.2 km.

The trails pass through open fields and hardwood areas. Two are loop trails, one the "Rideau Trail" is on the Rideau Walking Trail and must be travelled both ways. For beginners mostly. Map at parking lot or free from Ontario Ministry of Natural Resources, Box 239, Lanark, Ont.

Carillon Provincial Park
LOCATION: 17 km east of Hawkesbury on Hwy. 417.
LENGTH: Loop trails of 8 km.

680 ha of wooded and open gently rolling terrain in a natural state along south shore of Ottawa R. Lookout located at Carillon Dam. Ice travel on Ottawa R. not recommended due to fluctuating water

levels. This is a provincial park and maps are available at park office. Accommodation in Hawkesbury.

Larose County Forest
LOCATION: East of Ottawa about 48 km and 8 km north of Casselman. From Hwy. 417 take Limoges Exit.

County forest of about 10 400 ha with 400 ha reserved for cross-country skiers. Much of the rest is used by snowmobilers, who have 160 km of trails. Snowshoeing. Maps from Ministry of Natural Resources, Box 10, Bourget, Ont.

20 Upper Ottawa Valley

Forest Lea Trail
LOCATION: Off Forest Lea Rd. 13 km west of Pembroke.
LENGTH: 7 km of trails in three loops of 2-3 km or 30 to 60 min. average travel time.

This series of trails runs through pine and spruce plantations in a forest management area. Trail is maintained. Picnic tables along trail and toilets at parking area. Trail brochures at the registration box or from the Ministry office in Pembroke.

Nangor Cross-Country Resort
LOCATION: From Pembroke 8 km east on Hwy. 17, then 29 km northeast on County Roads 21 and 12. From Westmeath 8 km to northeast.
LENGTH: Four loops of 2, 2.2, 5 and 8.2 km. Links and connections give variety of 10 trails from 1 to 8.2 km. Unlimited off-trail skiing. All abilities.

The trails are in 160 ha of woodland with hills of 7 to 9 metres. Some skiing on bay with ice normally safe from December to March. Abundant wildlife. Trails overlook Laurentian Hills. Lighted skating rink, moonlight skiing, lessons, snowshoeing, babysitting, snowmobiles prohibited. Dining room with lounge and fireplace. Accommodation at Nangor Lodge for 56 persons. Trail maps at lodge or write Nangor Lodge, Westmeath, Ont. K0J 2L0.

Petawawa Forest Station Trails
LOCATION: From Chalk River south 6.5 km on station access road.
LENGTH: 50 km in a network of 7 trails plus connections.

Petawawa Forest Experiment Station of the Canadian Forestry Service has opened its large forest area to cross-country skiers. Many trails have been marked along fire control roads and others blazed by skiers.

Trails are color coded and one is marked with signs explaining forest ecology and forestry operations at research station. No regular grooming. Station advises that terrain is not generally difficult but skiers should travel in groups and treat this as a wilderness outing and carry map and compass. Various access points from road. Map available at station or write for maps and information to: C.E. Van Wagner, Canadian Forestry Service, Petawawa Forest Experiment Station, Chalk River, Ont. K0J 1J0.

Silver Spoon
LOCATION: Eastern edge of Deep River, near Ottawa R. From Hwy. 17 east on Town Line Rd., then southeast on Pembroke-Mattawa Rd. about 500 m and park on south side of road.
LENGTH: 14 km, about 2-3 hr, in five loops ranging from 1.5 to 5 km.

Site of Silver Spoon Grand Prix ski race, part of Silver Spoon Festival, traditionally held second weekend in February. Race draws several hundred competitors from recreational skiers to Olympic racers and is considered a preliminary for many who enter Canadian Ski Marathon at end of February. The trails run through woods and at places give good views of Ottawa R. and Laurentian Hills. Trails marked and maps posted at loop intersections. Loops run north and south of road, along Kennedy's Cr. and to edge of Ottawa R., crossing clearings, bridges and some open fields. For inexperienced to average ability. Maintained by club members. Lodging in Deep River.

3-M Ski Trail
LOCATION: West end of Deep River, starting at the local Mount Martin Ski Hill.
LENGTH: 5 km. Travel time 1 hr.

3-M ski trail (Mount Martin McAnulty) varies from wooded to open terrain and is very undulating but safe for skiers of all abilities. It has been designed as a race course for local program and is safe under even icy conditions. Fine views of the Ottawa R. and the Laurentian Hills. Mount Martin Ski Club maintains a small chalet at top of ski hill. Downhill facilities. Maps available in chalet. Local time trial races held most Saturday afternoons. Trail maintained by local ski enthusiasts. Accommodation in Deep River.

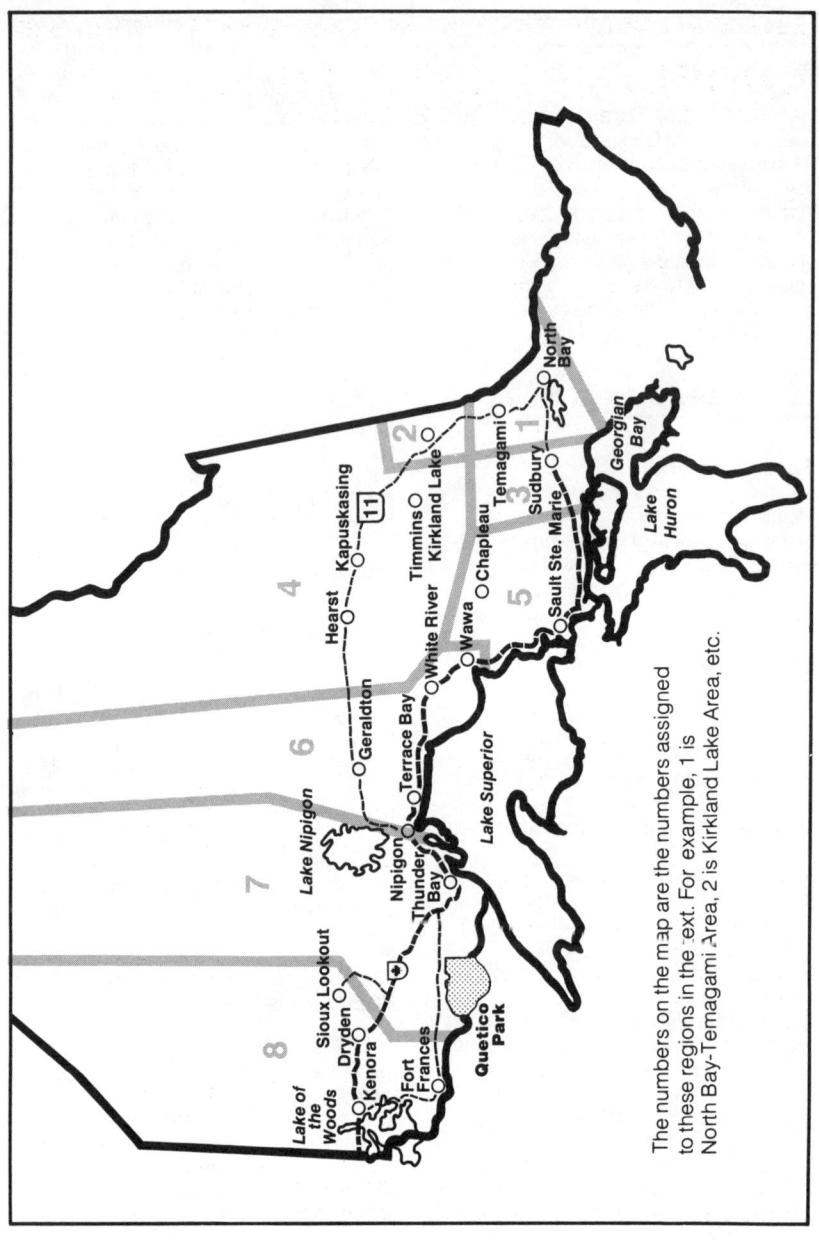

Northern Ontario Trails

1 North Bay – Temagami Area

North Country Trails
LOCATION: East of North Bay. Three main access points are at L'Auberge des Pionniers on Hwy. 17, west of Mattawa; Camp Conewango, on L. Talon; and Phelps Community Centre, just off Hwy. 63.
LENGTH: 200 km trail network.

One of the largest and best trail networks on the continent has been developed by the North Bay Area Cross-Country Ski Agency. This non-profit group tied together and expanded three smaller ski areas in a 402-square-kilometre bush area east of North Bay and north of the Mattawa R. It is an area of isolated lakes, beaver pasture, rugged cliffs, wild rivers, frozen waterfalls and tunnels formed by snow-clad spruce trees.

Trails are marked and are groomed daily by equipment designed by agency members. The ski season here runs from as early as the end of November to well into April and special plows that scoop snow back onto the trails keep routes open as long as possible. Trails are designed for all levels of skiers and some of the routes are specially designed and track set for members of Canada's racing teams. There are extensive possibilities for experienced skiers to explore the wilderness, climb the hills and make telemark turns in the deep snow. Wildlife in area includes deer and moose. Lessons, rentals, sales of equipment available from several outlets.

The ski agency makes a great effort to attract skiers from the south to stay for ski weeks or weekends. It books all travel and accommodation through its members and skiers can board The Northlander train in Toronto's Union Station and be transported to and around North Bay and to the ski trails as part of the package. For maps and extensive details write North Bay Area Cross-Country Ski Agency, Box 722, North Bay, Ont. P1B 1H0 or phone (collect) (705) 476-4700.

High Lake Trails
LOCATION: 8 km from downtown North Bay. From Hwy. 63 turn right on Peninsula Rd. then left on North Shore Rd. to reach clubhouse of North Bay Nordic Ski Club.
LENGTH: 30 km.

Four loop trails range through hilly, scenic terrain in predominantly hardwood forest. On longest loop there are lookouts over Trout L. and L. Nipissing. There is a 1.5 km beginner trail. The loops of 5, 8 and 16 km require ability to climb and descend hills under control. The trails, maintained by the ski club with assistance from the Ministry of Natural Resources, are open weekends. Snack bar on weekends. Site of annual Canadian Ski Association-sanctioned race in early February. For more information contact: North Bay Nordic Ski Club, Box 1524, North Bay, Ont. P1B 8K6.

Laurentian Ski Club
LOCATION: In city of North Bay.
LENGTH: About 5 km.

North Bay skiers have a combination cross-country and downhill ski area at their doorsteps. Part of loop trail system is on ski club property and part in adjacent forest. Climbs rolling, forested hills and provides excellent views over city and L. Nipissing. Lights for downhill night skiing illuminate some of the cross-country trails. Guided tours weekends. Ski school, rentals and food.

Larocque's Maple Sugar Shack
LOCATION: Northern outskirts of North Bay, off Cedar Heights Rd. just east of Gormanville Rd.
LENGTH: 6 km.

This is a long, loop trail, which can easily be broken into smaller loops by cutting over to the return track early. The Sugar Shack is located southeast of the intersection and the trail crosses Cedar Heights Rd. and runs parallel to Gormanville Rd.

Mattawa Wild River Area
LOCATION: Along Mattawa R., east of North Bay from Trout L. to Samuel De Champlain Provincial Park.

The two parks along this beautiful, wild river, a major route of the voyageurs and explorers, comprise 5600 ha of rugged

Northern Ontario countryside. Skiing on trails, particularly portage trails used by canoeists in summer. Snowshoeing. Snowmobiling on park roads only. This is wild country, though it lies just north of Hwy. 17, and should be treated as such by anyone planning extensive travel.

Nipissing Ridge Ski Area

LOCATION: South of North Bay. From Powassan go west on Hwy. 534 for 3 km then south on Ski Hill Rd. for another 3 km.
LENGTH: 15 km over three trails.

This resort, which also has downhill skiing, has cross-country trails of 1 and 4 km. The second trail connects to the Balla Hill Development Rd., which allows another 10 km of skiing. The area is wooded and trails are rated by the area as easy. Instruction, rentals, food, babysitting available. Resort open Friday through Sunday and on holidays. For more information write: Nipissing Ridge Ski Area, RR 1, Callander, Ont. P0H 1H0.

John P. Webster Nature Preserve

LOCATION: From Powassan, south of North Bay, go west about 16 km on Hwy. 534.
LENGTH: 8 km of loops.

This 130 ha property, under development, has skiing on two loops of nature trails. The routes pass a small lake, wetlands, a pine plantation and mixed forests. For detailed information on access and on the reserve contact the North Bay-Mattawa Conservation Authority, Box 1215, North Bay, Ont. P1B 3W7.

Eau Claire Gorge

LOCATION: East of North Bay about 50 km. From Hwy. 17 go south on Hwy. 630 in direction of Kiosk.

This conservation authority area is under development in the rugged country just north of Algonquin Park. The Amable du Fond R., which drains Kioshkokwi L. into the Mattawa R., flows between steep, rock walls in a series of rapids and waterfalls. The access road and some nature trails are suitable for skiing but other hiking trails are too steep. For more detailed information on access and on the area contact the North Bay-Mattawa Conservation Authority, Box 1215, North Bay, Ont. P1B 3W7.

Thorne Ski Resort

LOCATION: On south edge of Thorne along Ottawa R. near Temiscaming, Que.
LENGTH: Series of loop trails totalling 30 km with plans to expand this greatly.

The ski resort is located west from Hwy. 63 just south of the town. The trails start from chalet, also used for a small downhill area, and wind out through the bush country and over small streams. Variety of wooded and open areas with hills. Rentals, trail grooming, cookout areas, night skiing and snowshoeing. Map free at the chalet. Site of annual Thorne-Temiscaming Ski Club annual races with classic combination of events: cross-country, jumping, slalom and downhill. For more information write: Thorne Ski Resort, Thorne, Ont. P0H 2J0

Tri-Town Ski Village

LOCATION: South of Haileybury, New Liskeard and North Cobalt. From North Cobalt go south on Hwy. 567 (Lorraine Valley Rd.) for 13 km.
LENGTH: 25 km of loops.

Trails for all levels of skiers run through wooded area just west of L. Timiskaming. Cross-country area shares base chalet with downhill resort, and nordic skiers sometimes use poma lift to get to higher areas. There is a 120 m vertical rise. Groomed and track set nordic trails pass three small lakes and a number of viewpoints over the surrounding bush. Food and maps at area. Trail fees. Races and after-ski parties held during the winter. For more information phone (705) 672-3888.

Camp Wanapitei

LOCATION: From Temagami 29 km by ski plane or by Milne Lumber Co. forest road.
LENGTH: Unlimited possibilities in wilderness with a number of regular trails on paths, portage trails, abandoned logging roads and frozen waterways.

Camp Wanapitei dates back to the early part of the century as a canoe camp, particularly for young people, and is one of the better known ones in Ontario. Staff members always returned during the winter to cut and store ice for the summer season. At first they used snowshoes, but some acquired cross-country skis and from there came the idea of opening the camp for winter ski tours.

Trails of 30 km and longer are used for long day trips, and winter camping trips can be organized with staff as guides. Skiers must arrange accommodation in advance and can charter a small plane or drive to near camp and ski in last 1500 m. Lodging is in frame cabins heated by wood stoves. Skiers bring own sleeping bags, good for temperatures down to about 5 degrees Celsius, in addition to ski and touring equipment.

Skiers usually head out for trips with members of camp staff and carry lunch. Trails range from novice to expert and cross areas from flat to hilly and heavy bush to lightly treed. There is an unlimited opportunity for bushwhacking on skis or trying out snowshoes. At night skiers eat in dining cabin. Evenings tend to be convivial with singsongs, square dances and parties. Room for 35 visitors.

The camp is normally opened during the mid and late March to cover the period of school breaks. If a group reserves ahead it can be opened other weekends. For information write: Bruce Hodgins, 7 Engleburn Pl., Peterborough, Ont.

Temagami Area Trails

LOCATION: A network of trails radiating from central area of eastern shore of L. Temagami near town of Temagami.
LENGTH: Range from less than 1 km to about 25 km, providing trips of one-half hour to one day.

The trails are maintained by Temtoa (Temagami Tourist Operators' Association) a group of eight camps, six of which are open in the winter. Write the association in Temagami, Ont. for brochure of members and they will provide details of the trails. The routes wander over lakes, logging roads and portage trails through pure Canadian Shield country: boreal forest of red and white pine, cedar, spruce, fir, poplar and birch. Trails are varied. Camps will pack a lunch or provide a hot meal if you return at noon. Ice fishing for lake trout, whitefish and pickerel. Loon Lake Lodge, Temagami, Ont., has ski and snowshoe rentals and will provide instruction if requested in advance.

Temagami has long been a favorite summer recreation area, particularly for canoeists and fishermen. It is starting to develop as a winter sports area. The wilderness around the region offers extensive possibilities for wilderness tours and winter camping.

Finlayson Point Provincial Park

LOCATION: From Temagami south and west 1 km on Hwy. 11 and access road.
LENGTH: 3.5 km of loops.

Trails have been developed in this 30 ha recreation class provincial park on the south shore of the east arm of L. Temagami. Area is hilly and wooded in typical Shield country.

Headwaters Program

LOCATION: Temagami area.

Headwaters is an outfit that runs cross-country ski and snowshoeing trips through the frozen wilderness of Northern Ontario's Temagami region. The usual format is to bring groups in for one, two or three weeks and give people instruction not only in wilderness travel but in how to live in the Northern Ontario bush during winter. Some trips are for teachers or university students who are taking the program as an educational credit. The base camp is permanent but all groups spend at least two nights camping out. All equipment, including skis, winter clothing and sleeping bags, is provided. The travel is through heavy bush and across frozen lakes, with guides from the camp. For information write: Headwaters, Temagami, Ontario.

2 Kirkland Lake Area

Bear Rapids Hiking and Ski Trails

LOCATION: Swastika.

A small network of trails runs along the edge of Otto L. and the Blanche R. at Culver Park. Trails are maintained by the Kirkland Lake Recreation Dept. and map is available from the community complex.

Edgewood's Trails

LOCATION: Edgewood Restaurant, Kenogami L. At junction of Hwys. 11 and 66; just west of Kirkland Lake.
LENGTH: 16 km of loop trails.

Trails range from a series of beginner loops beside the restaurant to wilderness touring routes which demand skill and good judgment. These trails lead past spruce swamp, abandoned mines and sawmills, along cliffs, across rivers, down ravines and through forests. Many areas are inaccessible to snowmobiles and are packed by skiers or snowshoers. Groups regularly tour the area on weekends and hold cookouts and night skiing when the sky is clear. Guide available. Lessons coordinated by a certified instructor in cooperation with Northern College, Kirkland Lake campus. Rentals can be arranged through restaurant. Season is from early December to the end of April. Map available at restaurant for inner trails with wall map showing outer loops. Area covered by topographic map 42 A/1 and other maps of Kenogami L. basin area available from Ministry of Natural Resources, Mines Branch, Kirkland Lake. Third oldest winter carnival in Canada and the largest in Northern Ontario is held in Kirkland Lake at the end of February and a major ski race is run at the Edgewood's Trails. The region was settled by Finnish immigrants and cross-country skiing here goes back for many years. For information on trails write: Edgewood Restaurant, Kenogami Lake, RR 2, Site No. 4, Box 9, Swastika, Ont. P0K 1T0. For information on carnival write: Kirkland Lake Winter Carnival, Box 966, Kirkland Lake, Ont.

Kap-kig-iwan Provincial Park

LOCATION: South of Kirkland Lake. From Englehart south 3 km on park access road.
LENGTH: 5 km circuit from park entrance.

This attractive, 288 ha park on the Englehart R. is heavily forested with poplars and some hardwoods. Land is rolling with an attractive river valley and frequently steep banks. Park is known for very scenic High Falls and series of rapids upstream from the falls. Good photographic possibilities. Trail groomed. Site of Northeastern Regional Games. Maps available from Ministry of Natural Resources, Box 129, Swastika, Ont.

Larder Ski Club Trails

LOCATION: From Larder Lake south 2 km on Hwy. 624.
LENGTH: 9 km of loops.

This cross-country ski area starts from the ski chalet shared with a downhill area, which has a 55 m vertical rise. Cross-country loops of 6.5 and 2.5 km from chalet through wooded terrain. Trails marked with signs and blue ribbon. Map posted at chalet. Snack bar, ice fishing, snowmobile trails in vicinity.

Marter Valley Nordic Ski Centre

LOCATION: Northeast of Englehart. From Hwy. 11 go north on Hwy. 624 for 6 km to parking lot on east side of highway.
LENGTH: 5 km of loop trails with expansion planned.

The trail network is a project of the Englehart Nordic Ski Club. Basically the trails follow a ridge above the bank of the Wendigo R. with loops branching off to level ground. Groomed trails have double tracks and are marked for beginner to advanced skiers. The terrain varies from fir forest to open areas with new growth of firs. Wildlife includes rabbits, fox, grouse, grosbeaks and other native birds. Chalet is located on the banks of the river. The area is used for recreational skiing by area residents, training for students and for competition by local ski teams. On the east side of Hwy. 624 an additional 3.5 km of trails are available. Lodging in Englehart, Earlton and along Hwy. 11. For further information on the trails contact James Hamilton, Box 866, Englehart, Ont. P0J 1H0.

Otto Lake Hiking and Ski Trails

LOCATION: West of Kirkland Lake. Culver Park, Swastika.
LENGTH: 4.8 km, several loops, travel time 2 hr.

Trail wanders through rolling woodland. Wildlife in area. Scenic rapids can be seen from south side of trail. For lodging information, write Chamber of Commerce, Kirkland Lake. Maps available at Parks and Recreation Office, above Arena, Kirkland Lake, Ont.

Raven Mountain Ski Resort

LOCATION: From Kirkland Lake east 47.5 km on Hwy. 66.
LENGTH: Loop trails of .75, 2 and 4 km. One straight trail of 5 km.

All wooded trails with considerable slope. Some wildlife. Resort holds special events. Trails maintained. Downhill skiing. Accommodation available in Kirkland Lake. Contact Chamber of Commerce, Kirkland Lake or Bruce Morris, President, Raven Mountain Ski Club.

3 Sudbury Area

Cambrian College Ski Trail

LOCATION: Cambrian College, 1400 Barry Downe Rd., Sudbury.
LENGTH: 3 km loop.

This trail, which provides about a 30-minute run for recreational skiers, goes through wooded, slightly rolling terrain with some flat, open stretches. It is best suited for beginner and intermediate level skiers and for family outings. Rentals, instruction, field house with change rooms and refreshments. Showshoeing area nearby. The ski trail is a fitness trail in summer.

Killarney Provincial Park

LOCATION: South of Sudbury on north shore of Georgian Bay. From Hwy. 69 southwest on Hwy. 637.

Killarney is a uniquely beautiful area in Ontario. In addition to a generous sprinkling of lakes among its forests, it is traversed by the La Cloche Mountains, rising as much as 305 m above the surrounding countryside. These low mountain ranges of white quartz are spectacular as they rise precipitously from the shores of frozen lakes. The area has long been a favorite with artists, including members of the Group of Seven. One of its lakes is named OSA after the Ontario Society of Artists.

It is a beautiful land but also remote and wild, particularly in winter. Parties of cross-country skiers should be prepared for mountain-type skiing if they venture onto the high ground of steep cliffs and deep, snow-filled gullies. The area is very popular with canoeists in summer and it is possible to follow some canoe routes over lakes, rivers and portage trails when the waterways are well frozen. There is also a summer hiking trail, starting from the George Lake campground, but in many places it crosses steep ground and travel can be difficult on skis. Good map of the 34000 ha park available from sources including Parks Branch, Ministry of Natural Resources, Queen's Park, Ont.

Laurentian University Ski Club Trails

LOCATION: Laurentian University, Sudbury. Take Ramsey Lake Rd. then South Bay Rd. to Physical Education Centre. Trails start at Outdoor Centre.
LENGTH: 15 km of loop trails.

There are four trails ranging from a beginner's run around the playing fields to intermediate and advanced trails through rolling, semi-wooded terrain. This is a picturesque area with many lookout points over the Lake Laurentian Conservation Area. Instruction, rentals, trail grooming, ski shop, snack bar and night skiing. Maps at area. Trail fee.

Nordics Ski Club

LOCATION: Starts at Dowling Community Hall, town of Dowling.
LENGTH: Main trail is a 5 km loop with cut-off trails of 1, 2 and 3 km. Full trail takes 40 min. for average skier.

Dowling is 32 km northwest of Sudbury and trails are in area south and east of the town's community hall. The area is wooded with small conifers and hardwoods and the trails traverse some alder swamps. Arena near community centre has snack bar weekends and weekdays from 4-10 P.M. Skating in arena. Trails groomed. Open race late December or early January. Winter carnival race mid-February. Accommodation in town and area. Map available from Andy Ramta, President, Nordics Ski Club, Dowling, Ont. (send self-addressed, stamped envelope).

Voima Athletic Club Trails

LOCATION: Trails start from Voima Clubhouse on Sunnyside Rd., Sudbury.
LENGTH: About 60 km of loops.

This trail network, fanning out from the Finnish Canadian Athletic Association clubhouse, has routes ranging from 1 to 30 km. There are trails for beginner through advanced skiers. Trails are used for loppets, school meets, recreational races and for meets of provincial, national and international scope. Rentals, learn to ski program, breakfast and lunch in hall, with seating capacity of 300, showers, sauna, waxing area and kitchen. Maps and further information available from Voima Inc., RR 4, Site 35, Box 2, Sudbury or phone Sudbury and District Sports Central (705) 674-8900.

Walden Cross-Country Fitness Club

The Walden Cross-Country Fitness Club maintains a series of trails and has a program to revitalize interest in cross-country skiing in the area west of Sudbury. Beaver Lake, a small Finnish community, was a skiing centre in the 1920s and sent a number of competitors to provincial and national ski meets. After a lull in interest, cross-country skiing is again becoming a popular sport in the area. The club has five trails for skiing and running in the Beaver Lake, Lively and Naughton areas. It is promoting instruction and touring with a view to holding loppets and expanding the racing program beyond the secondary school level.

Beaver Lake Trails

LOCATION: Start from Beaver Lake Recreation Hall on Hwy. 17, 40 km west of Sudbury.
LENGTH: 4.5 km of loops.

From clubhouse, just west of Ella Rd., the trails start at the athletic field and run south through forest and fields. The 2.5 km loop is rated moderately difficult but the 2 km extension includes some steep sections that provide lookouts and challenge for advanced skiers. The trail is also a fitness trail and a nature trail in summer.

Camp Wassakwa
LOCATION: From Sudbury west about 60 km to Bass L.
LENGTH: Trails of 2.5 and 5 km.

Trails are used for skiing, conditioning and horseback riding at this day camp.

Naughton Sport Centre Trails
LOCATION: Naughton, 25 km west of Sudbury on Hwy. 17.
LENGTH: Trails of 1, 2 and 5 km.

This network has trails ranging from easy to difficult. They start from parking lot by ball park at end of Laura St. near the start of a snowmobile trail. Ski trails include easy, flat land; bush trail with moderate climbs; and longer trails with difficult up and downhill sections. This area has a 1 km lighted section for night skiing.

Anderson's Farm
LOCATION: Lively Village, 16 km west of Sudbury on Hwy. 17.
LENGTH: Trails of 1 and 2 km.

Has lighted trails for night skiing.

Lively School Trails
LOCATION: Lively District Secondary School.
LENGTH: 7.5 km.

This series of loops within loops contains everything from easy to difficult sections as it winds through bush, swamp, fields, across hills and along streams. It is located at edge of the school and passes through golf club and in one section passes near the Walden Industrial Park.

4 Timmins – Hearst Area

Clear Lake Trails
LOCATION: From Kapuskasing east 10 km on Hwy. 11 and Clear Lake Rd.
LENGTH: Five trails in loops of from 2.5 to 15 km with total of 35 km.

Trail head at chalet near edge of Clear L. Trails cross flat evergreen and swamp land containing grouse, rabbits, fox, moose, wolves, lynx and martens. Warm-up shelters, fireplaces and privies along the trails. Area used for time trials by Kap Nordic Skiers. For more information contact the club at 13 Kennedy St., Kapuskasing, Ont.

Hearst Cross-Country Ski Club
LOCATION: From Hearst north 4.8 km on Hwy. 583.
LENGTH: About 16 km of double set tracks.

All trails are about 3.5 m wide, double lane, identified with painted blazes on trees, distances marked, groomed. Flat to gently rolling terrain with various timber types. All water crossings bridged. Two shelters, coffee in main shelter (1 P.M. to 8 P.M.) picnic areas with firewood, picnic tables, cleared hill area, parking lots, outdoor privies. Monthly skiing night on Saturday nearest to full moon. For accommodation, write Hearst Board of Commerce, P.O. Box 1522, Hearst, Ont. Maps available on trails and panel board at main parking lot or through Board of Commerce.

Kettle Lakes Provincial Park
LOCATION: From Timmins east 32 km on Hwy. 101, then north 3.2 km on Hwy. 67.
LENGTH: 3 and 6 km loop trails. Maximum travel time 2 hr.

Wooded gentle to flat terrain, ideal for beginners. Marked trail system. Open picnic shelter on 6 km loop. Privies. Accommodation in Timmins area.

Mattagami Ski Trail
LOCATION: From Smooth Rock Falls, north on Hwy. 807.
LENGTH: About 8 km.

Wooded, very hilly terrain, following the banks of the Mattagami R. Narrow scenic trail, one of the most challenging in area. Open whenever snow permits. Trail marked. Warm-up cabin. Ice fishing at Legault's L. Accommodation in Smooth Rock Falls.

Porcupine Ski Runners Trails
LOCATION: In Timmins, 4 km east of city centre and just east of Schumacher on Hwy. 101.
LENGTH: Just over 16 km of loop trails.

Four trails, beginner, intermediate and advanced, are cut through rolling, wooded terrain. Trails are groomed and track set by the club. Food, lodging, rentals and instruction can be obtained in Timmins. Area is used for James Bay Frontier Touring Championships, a recreational event for skiers during the Timmins Winter Carnival each February. Ski races also held on trails. Maps available at trails or from Lorne Luhta, Box 973, Schumacher, Ont. P0N 1G0.

Remi Lake Provincial Park

LOCATION: East of Kapuskasing. From Hwy. 11 just west of Moonbeam go north on Hwy. 581 for about 3 km.
LENGTH: 11 km of loops.

Trails for all levels of skiers are located in wooded, rolling terrain. Cross-country and downhill ski area with 40 m vertical rise share common ski chalet, which is open only when downhill area is operating. Chalet has ski rentals and food. Warm-up shelter is located on cross-country trails, which are always open. Maps at main chalet and in trail register boxes. For more information contact Ministry of Natural Resources, 6-8-10 Government Rd., Kapuskasing, Ont. P5N 2W4.

Sturgeon Cross-Country Area

LOCATION: Trail at edge of Kapuskasing. Parking lot off Kimberly Dr. by Kapuskasing R.
LENGTH: Two trails of 7.5 and 12 km.

Parts of the trail run along the scenic riverbank, climbing gullies and passing through mixed forests. It is close enough that people from the town can ski to it from their homes. For more information and map, contact the Kap Nordic Skiers, 13 Kennedy St., Kapuskasing, Ont.

5 Algoma – Sault Area

Fort Creek Conservation Area

LOCATION: Geographic centre of Sault Ste. Marie. Runs north from Hwy. 550 (Second Line), 2.5 km west of Hwy. 17.
LENGTH: 4 km of trails on 72 ha.

This wooded ravine park in the heart of a major city is within walking distance of many residents. It is used year-round for such activities as skiing, snowshoeing, hiking, canoeing and nature study. Ski trails groomed. There is a network of trails, including a fitness trail with exercise equipment. Vegetation study stations have been established.

The natural forest covering the headwaters of the Fort Creek is located at about a 274 m elevation at the foot of the Prince Landscape and runs 5 km through watershed ravines to dam at margin of Algonquin Terrace. Flood control dam has created large reservoir. From there Korah Bench marks drop to Nipissing Terrace and older parts of city. For winter, a warm-up hut can be used by contacting Sault Ste. Marie Conservation Authority, 99 Foster Dr., Civic Centre.

Hiawatha Park and Crystal Creek Conservation Area

LOCATION: From Sault Ste. Marie north 5 km on Hwy. 17, then east 5 km on Fifth Line Rd.
LENGTH: A trail network from Sault Finnish Ski Club lodge. Trails of 2, 4, 5 and 10 km. Terrain varied with flat land and easy hills on short trails and more difficult terrain for longer runs. Hardwoods and some red pine reforestation. The Finnish club has a big lodge of logs and has snack bar, fireplace, saunas and dance floor. Trails groomed and tracks set by machine. Club organizes a race in mid-winter and wilderness tours for members. Map posted in lodge. Accommodation in Soo. Contact Chamber of Commerce, Sault Ste. Marie, Ont.

Stokely Creek Lodge

LOCATION: From Sault Ste. Marie north on Hwy. 17 for 32 km then right on Buttermilk Rd. for just over 3 km to signs.
LENGTH: More than 80 km in eight trails.

The lodge is located at the foot of 580 m King Mt. in Algoma hill country near the edge of L. Superior. In addition to the groomed trails, there are endless kilometres of wilderness skiing for the adventurous and expert skier. The area receives about 270 cm of snow in winter. There is one beginner and one expert trail. The others are rated intermediate and pass through maple bush and beside four small lakes. Rentals, guide service, food and accommodation at the area or in Sault Ste. Marie. For information: Stokely Creek Lodge, Karalash Corners, Goulais River, Ont. P0S 1E0. Phone (705) 649-3421.

Kwagama Lake Lodge

LOCATION: Near edge of Lake Superior Provincial Park in the Algoma region. To reach the lodge you must make reservations and take the Algoma Central Railway Snow Train from Sault Ste. Marie north 190 km then ski 13 km into the bush. Luggage is taken by snowmobile.

LENGTH: There are groomed trails of 8, 14 and 15 km to a nearby lake, Kwagama Mt. and the rim of the Agawa Canyon and back to the lodge. Extensive possibilities for wilderness exploring for the expert skier.

This retreat, a fly-in fishing lodge by summer and a ski-in lodge by winter, is a base for some of the finest wilderness skiing in Ontario. The Algoma region is one of the most scenic in the province and from the top of the 700 m bald Kwagama Mt. you can look over L. Superior on one side and forested hills and valleys on the other. Skiers coming to the lodge should have at least enough experience to feel comfortable in deep snow. The lodge is run by Mac and Grace MacEwan and skiers stay in rustic cabins. There is a shower, sauna and dining room with fireplace. Skiers come either for long weekends or for a week. For further information write: Kwagama Lake Lodge, 176 Manitou Dr., Sault Ste. Marie, Ont. P6B 5L1 or phone (705) 253-3075.

Lake Superior Provincial Park

LOCATION: On east shore of L. Superior between Sault Ste. Marie and Wawa.

This is a 1300 sq. km park that is a favorite with wilderness touring skiers and snowshoers. Snowmobiles are prohibited. The country is mountainous and remote and skiers planning long trips should be well equipped. The Ministry of Natural Resources, Box 1160, Wawa, Ont. has topographic maps available and lists two trails. The Mijin-Old Woman Lake Trail starts from Hwy. 17 at Mijin Lake Access Rd., about 32 km south of Wawa and the Gargantua Trail starts at Gargantua Rd., about 40 km south of Wawa. There are hundreds of kilometres of logging roads. The area is in the Algoma region, a rugged and highly scenic part of Ontario favored by members of the Group of Seven Canadian painters. There are high cliffs and wild rivers and the spectacular Agawa Canyon, site of excursion train rides on Algoma Central Railway. Accommodation along Hwy. 17 and in Wawa.

Voyageur Trail

LOCATION: A 400 km trail for hiking, cross-country skiing and snowshoeing from South Baymouth on Manitoulin I. to Gros Cap, west of Sault Ste. Marie. Runs along north shore of L. Huron.

This ambitious trail project was started in 1973 by a group of northern residents with some help from Southern Ontario hikers, including members of the Bruce Trail Assn. The Voyageur route is seen as an extension of the Bruce, picking up across Georgian Bay from the tip of the Bruce Peninsula. It passes through such north shore communities as Little Current, Espanola, Spanish, Blind River, Thessalon and the Soo, then ends 40 km further west at a rock promontory in L. Superior. Long range plans call for it to push east to the Ottawa Valley and northwest across the top of L. Superior as a major link in what could become a transcontinental trail series starting with the Appalachian in Georgia and ending with the Pacific Crest in Baja California.

Only some parts of the Voyageur have been completed and not all areas are suited for skiing as the country is very rugged. It wanders through hemlock forests, crosses many streams, skirts lakes and beaver ponds and climbs the glistening, white quartz hills of the La Cloche range just west of Killarney. For much of its length, the trail passes along a very rugged escarpment, twisting and turning to avoid major natural obstacles. In many areas blue blazes indicate side trails to points of interest and lookouts. Main trail is marked with white blazes, like the Bruce Trail. Every 500 m there are blue on yellow, diamond-shaped markers to indicate distance travelled. Numerous access points are marked with green and white signs.

Like the Bruce, this trail is being built by local clubs along its length and much of it crosses private land. Users are asked to respect this fact. Since this is dense wilderness in most places, skiers should be in parties experienced in and equipped for such travel. Map and compass necessary. For information and details on what parts of the trail are usable, contact Voyageur Trail Assn., Box 66, Sault Ste. Marie, Ont.

Chapleau Ski Club

LOCATION: Starting point at the Chapleau Ski Hill on the north side of town.
LENGTH: 11 km. Travel time 3 hr.

Easy trail, for beginners, located in heavily wooded area with some open spaces. Downhill facilities, snack bar. For accommodation, write Chamber of Commerce, Chapleau, Ont. Free map available from Chapleau Ski Club.

6 North Shore Area

Greta Road, Aeroplane Lake Trail
LOCATION: From Geraldton go north on Hwy. 584 for about 8 km then west on Greta Lake Rd. for 4 km to trail head.
LENGTH: Trail is rated at one to three hours return trip time depending on conditions and skier.

This trail is through gently rolling, wooded terrain and is rated as good for novice skiers. There is a chance of spotting tracks or wildlife along the way. Maps available from Ministry of Natural Resources, Box 640, Geraldton, Ont. P0T 1M0 or phone (807) 854-1030.

Otter Slide Ski Club
LOCATION: West of Geraldton. From Longlac west 21 km on Hwy. 11.
LENGTH: 15 km.

From the club chalet trails loop out through lightly to heavily wooded area. They cross flat areas, gently rolling terrain with several small hills and one small lake. Intermediate ability required. Cookouts. The area also has a small downhill run which operates rope tows on weekends. Trail fees for non-members of club. Maps posted on trails.

Lahti Road Ski Trail
LOCATION: From Geraldton west 2.5 km on Hwy. 11.
LENGTH: The road runs south from Hwy. 11 and skiers go more than 20 km to the Kimberly Clark access road. Round trip to return to highway is about six hours if conditions are good.

Local skiers regularly use this road and trappers use it as an access route to their traplines. The route varies from flat to gently rolling, wooded terrain, which skirts lakes, rivers, eskers, and swamps. Road is marked on 1:250,000 topographic map, Longlac 42 E, Edition 2.

Wawa Ski Club
LOCATION: From Wawa south 4 km on Hwy. 17.
LENGTH: 10 km in network of six loops.

Trails begin near Ontario Provincial Police station and wind though wooded and gently sloping country. This is in the highly scenic Algoma region and trail system is north of Lake Superior Provincial Park and just south of the summer resort town of Wawa. Topographic maps 41 N/10, 41 N/15, and 42 C/2 cover the area.

Picnic Lake Ski Trail
LOCATION: Just east of White R. on Hwy. 631 (1.8 km from junction with Hwy. 17).
LENGTH: 3.4 km loop which takes about one-half hour to complete.

This trail, maintained by the Ministry of Natural Resources, passes a series of small ponds just east of Picnic L. Parking lot at start of trail.

Nordic Ski Trail
LOCATION: Between Schreiber and Terrace Bay off Hwy. 17.
LENGTH: 6.4 km loop trails plus 2 km non-loop trail.

This area has three loops plus one trail which does not loop, close to the cliffs along the rugged L. Superior shoreline. Lookouts provide spectacular views. Trails are in a mixed coniferous-deciduous forest typical of Superior's north shore and range through jack pine flats to rolling and even hilly country. Small animals and birds inhabit the area. Picnic table at rest stop and lookout. Trails groomed and maintained by Ministry of Natural Resources. Fixed maps on trails. Pocket maps and further information from Ministry of Natural Resources, Box 280, Terrace Bay, Ont. P0T 2W0.

Rainbow Falls Provincial Park
LOCATION: From Schreiber west 12 km on Hwy. 17.
LENGTH: About 5 km of trails plus skiing on lake and on summer access roads.

The Ministry of Natural Resources keeps a parking lot plowed at this 569 ha summer camping park. Skiers follow park roads and ski on Selim L. when the ice is safe. Side trails lead to lookouts over L. Superior's rugged shoreline. Scenic waterfalls on Selim R. Picnic tables and barbecues. Area is heavily wooded with young deciduous and coniferous forests. Park road map and information available from Ministry of Natural Resources, Box 280, Terrace Bay, Ont. P0T 2W0.

Rendez-Vous Ski Trail
LOCATION: From Nipigon west 5 km then follow Golf Course Rd. 500 m to start of trail.
LENGTH: 6 km loop with several interconnecting side trails.

Trail runs through mixed forest and cedar stand with gentle hills and short side trails to more demanding hills. The Rendez-vous Cross-Country Ski Club rents a chalet at the start of the trail most Sundays and holds socials monthly. Refreshments and snacks in the afternoon followed by pot luck suppers and local musicians. Skiers travelling the Trans-Canada Highway are welcomed. Trails groomed periodically by club. Equipment and accommodation in Nipigon. Map at chalet or from Les's Cycle and Sport, Box 807, Nipigon, Ont. or Ministry of Natural Resources, Nipigon, Ont.

7 Thunder Bay – Quetico Area

Candy Mountain
LOCATION: About 25 km southwest of Thunder Bay. Take Hwy. 61 south, turn north on Hwy. 130 for 1.5 km then west on sideroad for 3 km to parking lot.
LENGTH: 12 km.

Candy Mountain Resorts Ltd. runs both a cross-country and a downhill ski resort. The start of the cross-country trails require a 100 m climb, which can be avoided by taking a T-bar ride. Aside from a teaching area and a small practice trail the system is a series of loops through wooded area on top of hills. Area has such wildlife as moose, wolves, fox and rabbits, but most skiers see only the tracks. Trails groomed and partly set with double tracks. Patrol on weekends, teaching, some rentals. Cookout area and food at ski chalot. Downhill area has vertical rise of more than 200 m. For information and map contact Candy Mountain Resorts Ltd., RR 6, Thunder Bay, Ont. P7C 4T9 or phone (807) 939-6033.

Centennial Park
LOCATION: Thunder Bay. From Hwy. 17-11 E. go south on Hodder Ave., then west on Arundel St. to Centennial Park Rd.
LENGTH: Trail system includes 5 and 10 km racing trails and touring trails including one to Cascades Conservation Area, 10 km away.

Trails for all abilities. Hilly and winding trails in forest area around park. Skiers cautioned to use trails since ice on Current R. can be hazardous. All-night skiing at Trowbridge Falls Park to north along river. Parking. Some trail grooming by clubs and Ministry of Natural Resources.

Sleigh rides, toboggan hill, some downhill skiing, skating on Boulevard L. Races organized by Thunder Bay Ski Club, Box 1085, Thunder Bay, Ont. and Reipas Sports Club, 879 John St., Thunder Bay. Lessons available to club members. Lodge, food. Maps on site and from City Parks and Recreation Department, 141 South May St., Thunder Bay, Ont. P7E 5V3. Lodging information from Visitors and Convention Bureau, 193 Arthur St., Thunder Bay, Ont.

Cascades Conservation Area
LOCATION: In northeast section of Thunder Bay. From Hwy. 17, then Balsam St. N. to end.
LENGTH: Two main ski trails totalling 3.7 km plus some small hiking trails on 141 ha park.

This park contains a variety of flora and fauna including large white pine. Excellent views of the Current R. from rocky outcrops. It was named for a unique geological feature, a series of spectacular rapids which tumble down the river for 500 m. Trails are marked with colored, triangular signs. Parking, picnic tables, snowshoeing. The park is part of a chain of ski trails reaching from Centennial and Trowbridge Falls parks in the city to Wishart Conservation area in the north. Maintained by Lakehead Region Conservation Authority.

Wishart Conservation Area
LOCATION: North of Thunder Bay on Hwy. 17, then north on Onion Lake Rd.
LENGTH: 2 km on 210 ha.

This is part of a chain of parks leading from Thunder Bay and used for cross-country skiing. Tobogganing and snowmobiling. Maintained by Lakehead Region Conservation Authority.

Kamview Ski Area
LOCATION: Southern outskirts of Thunder Bay. Southwest on Hwy. 61, 10 km then north 1.6 km on 20th Sideroad to parking on west side.
LENGTH: Five loops totalling 15 km.

This cross-country ski area is in generally wooded terrain ranging from rolling to hilly. Some areas give good views of city of Thunder Bay, harbour and Kaministiquia R. valley. Maps in box at plowed parking area. Contact Ministry of Natural Resources, 435 James St. S., Box 5000, Thunder Bay, Ont. for details.

Kakabeka Falls Provincial Park
LOCATION: From Thunder Bay west 29 km on Hwy. 11.
LENGTH: About 8 km.

Series of trails follow park summer roads to campgrounds through slightly hilly terrain on south side of area. Highly scenic region where Kaministiquia R. pours over 39-metre-high falls, called the Niagara of the North. History of the area tells that Green Mantle, daughter of an Ojibway chief, was captured by a raiding party of Sioux and was forced to guide the invaders to her tribe. Instead, she led them down the river to the mighty falls. Just before the attackers were swept over the cataract to their death on the rocks below, Green Mantle escaped and swam to shore. Legend says her spirit floats in the thick mists in the gorge below the falls and that the noise one hears is the rumbled anger of the Sioux.

Prince and Jarvis Cross-Country Ski Area
LOCATION: Lake Superior shoreline south of Thunder Bay. From airport go south on Hwy. 61 for 31 km then east on Sturgeon Bay Rd. for 10 km to parking area.
LENGTH: 35 km of loops plus side trails.

This wild and scenic area is especially suited to intermediate and better skiers. Since it is some distance from civilization one should carry at least such things as a spare ski tip and light lunch. Three loop trails have travel times ranging from two to six hours, depending on snow conditions and skiers. Trails tend to be icy during March. Spectacular views over L. Superior from 80 m high cliff while side trail offers a view from close to double that height. Esker Canyon trail takes skiers for 1 km through a gorge with walls up to 60 m high. Trail groomed and maintained from mid-December to March by Ministry of Natural Resources. Maps available at trail register box at parking area or from Ministry of Natural Resources, 435 James St. S., Box 5000, Thunder Bay, Ont. P7C 5G6.

Retto Lake Ski Trails
LOCATION: From Thunder Bay north on Hwy. 527 for about 22 km.
LENGTH: 17 km of loops.

Three trails run through remote, wooded terrain with many steep uphill climbs followed by short, fast downhill runs. This area is suited to intermediate and advanced skiers. From several of the hills there are good lookouts over small lakes and the wooded countryside. Trail is groomed by the Thunder Bay Ski Club, Box 1085, Station F, Thunder Bay, Ont. Maps from Ministry of Natural Resources, 435 James St. S., Box 5000, Thunder Bay, Ont. P7C 5G6.

Sibley Park Trails
LOCATION: Sibley Provincial Park. From Thunder Bay east on Hwy. 11 and 17 for 40 km to Hwy. 587, then south to park entrance.
LENGTH: About 50 km, 4 trails.

Sibley Park, located on a large peninsula jutting south into L. Superior, is a very scenic area. The high cliff at the south end has been dubbed the Sleeping Giant for its shape. Cross-country and snowshoeing trails wander between lakes and streams, generally following summer park roads. They are groomed depending on use. One trail runs between two points on Hwy. 587, another forms a loop around L. Marie Louise and two others skirt the Sleeping Giant formation. Contact Ministry of Natural Resources, 435 James St. S., Box 5000, Thunder Bay, Ont. P7C 5G6. Map available.

Sandbar Lake Trails
LOCATION: North Quetico Park. From Ignace on Hwy. 17 go north on Hwy. 599 to Sandbar Lake Provincial Park.
LENGTH: Loop trails ranging in length from 2 to 7 km.

This 3115 ha recreation class park has trails winding through wooded areas and past three small lakes. They are rated as family skiing routes with good scenery and chance of seeing wildlife. Trails groomed. Area is used for ski events by the Ignace Ski Club. For map and more information contact the Ministry of Natural Resources, Box 448, Ignace, Ont. P0T 1T0.

Mink Lake Trail
LOCATION: From Atikokan east 40 km on Hwy. 11 to Dawson Trail Campgrounds, at east entrance of Quetico Provincial Park. Entrance on north side of highway.
LENGTH: 3 loops ranging from 5 km (45 min.) to 15 km (2 hr.).

Trail was established by Ministry of Natural Resources on old logging roads just north of famous Quetico Provincial Park. Trails are marked and groomed with a track setting machine after every snowfall. Snowmobiles prohibited. Area was formerly logged and trails are on rolling terrain with moderate hills. Suitable for all abilities and used by local schools. Free trail map from Ministry of Natural Resources, Atikokan, Ont. Area and contour maps available for a fee. Accommodation information from Atikokan Chamber of Commerce.

This trail lies just across the highway from Quetico, a favorite park with wilderness canoeists. It was the land of Ojibway trappers and route of the Voyageurs and the Dawson Trail, used by westbound settlers. Wildlife including eagle, wolf, moose and small mammals and birds. Park is not marked for skiing but has obvious possibilities for the well-equipped, touring skier. Canoeist's map available from Ministry of Natural Resources.

Jim Lake Trail

LOCATION: Just north of Quetico Provincial Park. From junction of Hwys. 11 and 11B at south edge of Atikokan go south on access road for 4.5 km.
LENGTH: 18 km of loops with expansion planned to 33 km.

Trails run through heavily wooded country in the highly scenic Quetico canoe country but skiers should avoid water crossings. Routes pass white birch ridges, jack pine stands, black spruce swamps and beaver ponds. Trails are not difficult but area is remote and can be very cold. Groomed by the Ministry of Natural Resources. In summer these routes are used for hiking. For maps and more information contact the Ministry of Natural Resources, Atikokan, Ont. P0T 1C0.

Ignace Cross-Country Ski Trail

LOCATION: From Ignace southeast on Hwy. 17, then north 13 km on Hwy. 599.
LENGTH: Loop trails of 7 km.

Located in rugged northern Ontario wilderness, near the English R. system. Groomed trails skirt three small lakes in wooded country. Accommodation in Ignace. Map available free from Ministry of Natural Resources, P.O. Box 448, Ignace, Ont. P0T 1T0.

8 Dryden – Fort Frances Area

Big Sawbill Lake Trail

LOCATION: East of Rainy L. From Fort Frances go east 32 km on Hwy 11 then north on Hwy. 812 (Manitou Access Road) to various trail access points.
LENGTH: 28 km main trail plus offshoots.

This wilderness trail in rugged, scenic country is for the experienced skier, although some of the short sections at the north end of the trail are suitable for less seasoned skiers. Main access points are two parking lots 21 km and 30 km north of Hwy. 11. There is also an access point for a cutoff loop about 3 km north of the south parking lot. Depending on conditions, the main trail can take two days to complete, making it a wilderness touring route for the well-equipped skier. At places the hills are steep. Some areas offer lake travel if conditions are suitable. Cedar and birch bush with hilly and swampy areas. This is big game country and there is a chance of seeing some animal tracks. Map and further information from District Office, Ministry of Natural Resources, 922 Scott St., Fort Frances, Ont. P9A 1J4.

Dryden Ski Club

LOCATION: From Dryden, north on Hwy. 601 for 11 km, then continue north on Reed Rd. for 9.5 km.
LENGTH: Trails of 4.6, 6.8, 8, 9.6 km. Minimum travel time from 20 to 66 minutes. Graded intermediate.

Gently rolling terrain with a few small rock outcrops. All trails are interconnected and through treed area inhabited by moose, deer and wolves. Ski club open on weekends and holidays. Lessons available. Downhill facilities. Food concession in ski chalet. Hills and trails patrolled by Canadian Ski Patrol. Accommodation available in Dryden. For further information contact Tourist Bureau, Dryden. Topographic maps available in the Ministry of Natural Resources office in Dryden. Annual club races held about the first weekend in March. Skiers also use Wabigoon L. and numerous snowmobile trails around the area.

Mount Evergreen Ski Club

LOCATION: From Kenora northeast 5 km on Airport Rd.
LENGTH: 4 loop trails from 4 to 13 km.

Beginner, intermediate and advanced trails. Canadian Shield offers wooded trails as well as gentle slopes (elevation up to 46 m). Open every weekend. Instruction available from certified instructors. Rentals, chalet with change area and cafeteria.

Trails groomed and marked, cookout, downhill slopes. Maps available. For accommodation information contact Tourist Reception Centre, Hwy. 17 W., Kenora, Ont. Club races in January, Kenora Carnival races in March.

Reef Point–Hopkins Bay Trails
LOCATION: Southern edge of Rainy Lake. From Fort Frances go east on Hwy. 11 for 16 km, then north on Reef Point Rd. and Hopkins Bay Rd.
LENGTH: About 12 km of trail plus skiing on Hydro line right of way.

There is a series of trails of 1.6 to 4 km off Reef Point and Hopkins Bay Roads. Ability range from beginner to skiers who are able to handle downhill runs in places. Terrain ranges from gentle to steep hills. Pine ridges, ash stands, cedar swamp and beaver ponds. Several entrance points. Rest spots along trails. For map and more information contact District Office, Ministry of Natural Resources, 922 Scott St., Fort Frances, Ont. P9A 1J4.

Rushing River Provincial Park
LOCATION: From Kenora east 26 km on Hwy. 17, then south on Hwy. 71 to park.
LENGTH: 14 km.

Trail follows unplowed summer road to campsites. Series of trails in bush and on summer roads on the north side of Dogtooth Lake. Rushing River is a 158 ha park bounded on three sides by Dogtooth L. and traversed by Rushing R. Free maps at area. The region has a variety of animals – wolves, moose or deer. Winter visitors can see the tracks of red fox, ermine, mink, otter and beaver. The dominant forest tree is the jack pine, seeded naturally after a forest fire burned over this area in the early 1900s.

About 7 500 years ago, this region was covered by Lake Agassiz, the last glacial lake. The rounded boulders in the park were deposited by the last glacier. The park bedrock belongs to the Canadian Shield. For more information contact: District Manager, Ministry of Natural Resources, Provincial Building, Kenora, Ont.

Sioux Lookout Trails
LOCATION: In town of Sioux Lookout. Main departure point at the curling arena on 3rd Ave.
LENGTH: Network of 3 trails forming 2 loops of 4.8 km each or one of 8 km. Pelican L. is accessible directly from the trails.

The unmarked trails keep to gentle, sloping valleys and are suitable for all levels of skiers. They pass through meadows and forests of spruce, pine, birch and poplar. For lodging information, write Sioux Lookout – Hudson Chamber of Commerce, Sioux Lookout, Ont. Topographical map: Sioux Lookout 52J, available at Ministry of Natural Resources, Sioux Lookout.

Appendix

Wind Chill Factors

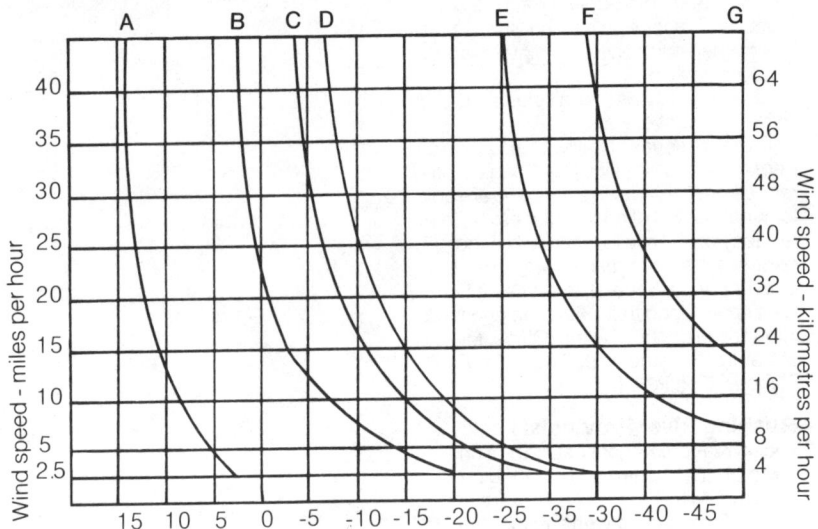

(A to B) Conditions considered comfortable when dressed for skiing.
(B to C) Conditions no longer pleasant for outdoor activities on overcast days.
(C to D) Conditions no longer pleasant for outdoor activities on sunny days.
(D to E) Freezing of exposed skin begins for most people depending on the degree of activity and the amount of sunshine.
(E to F) Exposed areas of the face freeze in less than 1 minute.
(F to G) Exposed flesh will freeze within half a minute for the average person.

Time Required to Ski a Given Distance at Different Speeds (hours and minutes)

		speed - miles per hour (kilometres per hour)						
		1.5 (2.4)	2.5 (4)	3.5 (5.6)	4.5 (7.2)	5.5 (8.8)	7.0 (11.2)	8.5 (13.6)	10 (16)
Distance in miles (kilometres)	1 (1.6)	40	24	17	13	11	8	7	6
	2 (3.2)	1.20	48	34	26	21	17	14	12
	3 (4.8)	2.00	1.12	52	40	32	25	21	18
	4 (6.4)	2.40	1.36	1.09	53	43	34	28	24
	5 (8)	3.20	2.00	1.27	1.06	54	44	35	30

Courtesy: Ben Buss

Speed of Travel in Different Activities

MPH	Snowshoeing	Hiking	Cross-Country Skiing	Running
10.00			Trained cross-country racer on a variety of trails and snow conditions.	Running hard.
8.50			Trained cross-country racer on a variety of trails and snow conditions.	Running hard.
7.00			Trained cross-country racer on a variety of trails and snow conditions.	Running.
5.50	Snowshoe jogging on packed or crusty snow by well-trained individual.		Pronounced kick and glide by touring skier on tracked trail. A racer working hard in unbroken snow.	Jogging.
4.50	Snowshoe jogging on packed or crusty snow by well-trained individual.	Stepping out vigorously on level, firm trail.	A touring skier showing gliding movements on tracked trail.	Light jogging.
3.50	Fast, well-trained individual travelling in deep snow.	Brisk walk on any trail.	Walking on skis with some gliding movements.	
2.50	An individual of average ability moving on hard trail or who has good technique in deep snow.	Slow walk.	Walking on skis in unbroken snow.	
1.50	Average or less ability in deep snow.	Ambling with young children.	Walking on skis with very young children.	

Courtesy: Ben Buss

Canadian Ski Association – Offices and Awards

One of the interesting things about cross-country skiing in Canada is the speed with which it has recently become so developed on a national basis. Clubs which had carried on for years with a hard core of devotees, often of Nordic extraction, suddenly started drawing members from the general public. New clubs have sprung up as skiers moved into areas where there was no organization, and many newcomers to the sport simply ski alone or with friends but are not affiliated with any organized body.

The nearest thing to an umbrella group for the sport is the cross-country section of the Canadian Ski Association. For many years this was a relatively small branch of the CSA and dealt mainly with competition. Now that the sport is gaining popular acceptance this branch is expanding and is taking an interest in the development of touring and events which attract a wide range of skiers.

The association is based in Ottawa but has representatives scattered across the country. In some areas there are permanent or semi-permanent offices, while in others CSA is represented by volunteers. A large number of ski clubs are affiliated with CSA.

The head office address is:

Canadian Ski Association
333 River Rd., Tower A
Ottawa, Ont. K1L 8B9

Local contacts where available can be obtained from the central office.

Among its activities the CSA awards emblems and plaques for ordinary skiers who are active enough in the sport to ski certain distances each year or fit enough to pass certain time trials. Detailed information on how to register for the events is available from the central or regional offices. Following is a summary of the distances and times for the awards.

Touring Distances for a Ski Season

Adults (17 and over)	Bronze	Silver	Gold
Men	200 km	400 km	750 km
Women	150 km	300 km	500 km
Juniors			
Age 7-9	40 km	100 km	150 km
Age 10-13	60 km	150 km	250 km
Age 14-16	100 km	200 km	400 km

Time Trial Awards Men 10 km	Bronze	Silver	Gold
Age 17-34	65 min.	56 min.	48 min.
Age 35-49	70 min.	62 min.	56 min.
Age 50 and over	100 min.	72 min.	64 min.
Women 5 km			
Age 17-34	40 min.	35 min.	27 min.
Age 35-49	45 min.	40 min.	35 min.
Age 50 and over	55 min.	50 min.	45 min.

Boys	**Bronze**	**Silver**	**Gold**
Age 7-9 (2.5 km)	30 min.	27 min.	25 min.
Age 10-13 (2.5 km)	23 min.	20 min.	17 min.
Age 14-16 (5 km)	34 min.	26 min.	23 min.
Girls			
Age 7-9 (2.5 km)	33 min.	30 min.	28 min.
Age 10-13 (2.5 km)	26 min.	22 min.	19:30 min.
Age 14-16 (5 km)	39 min.	33 min.	30 min.

Trail Signs

Markings for cross-country trails can vary widely. Sometimes there is just a path cut through the bush and the skier follows it relying on map and compass if the route is long or complicated. On organized trails there is often a splash of paint or a piece of orange surveyor's tape tied around a tree every so often along the route. Some trail developers have taken time to put name signs on pathways and even attempted to mark trails for the degree of difficulty.

A trail grading system often found in Ontario and based on an international code, is as follows:

green beginner

blue intermediate

red expert

Approximate Conversions to Metric

1 inch = 2.5 centimetres (cm)
1 yard = .9 metres (m)
1 mile = 1.6 kilometres (km)
1 square mile (640 acres) = 2.59 square kilometres (259 hectares [ha])

Celsius				
−40	−20	0	20	40
−40	−4	32	68	102
Fahrenheit				

Photograph Acknowledgements
Michael Keating viii, 7, 11, 12, 13, 14, 15, 22, 23, 28, 31, 35, 38, 41, 49, 53
Shelia Hirsch 33
Wilfried D. Schurig 56
Ontario Ministry of Industry and Tourism 59
Alberta Government Photograph x